MALABAR
FLORIDA 32950

THE

UNEQUAL ELITES_____

THE
UNEQUAL ELITES _____

ROBERT P. ALTHAUSER

Indiana University

SYDNEY S. SPIVACK

in collaboration with

BEVERLY M. AMSEL

Mt. Sinai School of Medicine

A WILEY-INTERSCIENCE PUBLICATION

JOHN WILEY & SONS, New York • London • Sydney • Toronto

Library of Congress Cataloging in Publication Data:

Althauser, Robert P   1939–
  The unequal elites.

  "A Wiley-Interscience publication."
  Bibliography: p.
  Includes index.
  1. Negro college graduates.   2. Educational
sociology—United States.   I. Spivack, Sydney
Shepherd, 1907–1969, joint author.   II. Title.

LC2781.A47   370.19'34   74-30497
ISBN 0-471-02524-0

Printed in the United States of America

10 9 8 7 6 5 4 3 2 1

To
Dorothy Dillon Spivack

FOREWORD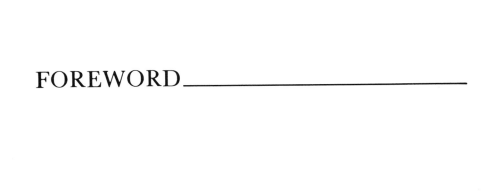

This inquiry into the differential impact of college on black and white graduates was conceived and initiated by the late Sydney Spivack, then jointly undertaken by Spivack and Robert Althauser, and then, upon Spivack's death, brought to completion by Althauser. The authors pursued this study as a limited test of their conviction that higher education can serve as a major instrument of social justice.

Spivack was one of those rare sociologists in whom all of the scholarly graces converged. He was at once the quintessential humanist—knowledgeable, comfortable with the sages, a connoisseur who took delight in literature and the arts—and an alert and skeptical social scientist with a tough-minded disdain for cant and for wishes disguised as reality. The sixties were a time when apocalyptic prophecies of protracted racial conflict were regularly advanced by both the political left and right. In that intellectual climate, Spivack maintained his confidence in several major propositions of the liberal's creed: native capacity is equally distributed among all racial groups; college is the principal mechanism for converting talent into career and status; a heightened moral sensibility and a prudent recognition of the conditions of national survival would lead American society to make education and its subsequent rewards accessible to black people, who have been among the most prominent victims of social injustice. Spivack rescued these sanguine expectations from conventional piety by his profound understanding of their root meaning, and by his insistence that his most cherished beliefs could survive only if they were sustained by disciplined social investigation.

At the very outset of the study the authors pose this question. "Do black and white men find that their resources, when equal, produce rewards of equal value in the marketplace of human competition?" Phrased in this way, this query suggests that the independent influence of graduation from college on careers can be determined only by adopting a quasi-experimental design in which other confounding variables governing the occupational achievement and income of blacks and whites can be controlled. Accordingly, the authors confined their analysis to the alumni of two predominantly white universities and one predominantly black institution of similar quality, and compared relatively small matched samples of their graduates between 1932 and 1964, with academic achievement and social class held constant. As the authors are scrupulous to say, these refinements are achieved at the expense of generalizability, and they make no claim for the extension of their findings to more recent periods or to other populations. Indeed, not the least of the virtues of this admirable study are the pains the authors take to acknowledge the limitations of their evidence. This much said, it is evident that the gains in specificity and precision altogether justify the authors' deliberate decision to limit the populations they study.

It is noteworthy, then, that Althauser has treated the data with a commendable mixture of virtuosity and restraint. His resourceful attention to methodological nicety, careful theoretical exposition, and sensitive discussion of policy, lead to conclusions that are more complex, hence more equivocal, than is customary in treatises on the relationship between education and careers. The findings will provide no comfort for those who are persuaded that "colleges make no difference" or for those who believe that higher education is the royal road to racial equality. The most general conclusion is that "in our moderately controlled comparison, an equal starting point was converted into one form of equal results—equal average job status. However, these equalities did not produce equal incomes, either median or average. The median income differences of roughly $500 favoring whites and, to a lesser extent, the $1500 difference (favoring whites) between white and Frazier [the predominantly black institution] black graduates are smaller than figures from previous (though not exactly comparable) analyses using 1960 Census data." These findings are sometimes substantially modified by other measures of income, regional variations, and by salary differentials in the public and private sectors, and by a great array of individual, social, and educational characteristics. Thus each year of graduate education beyond the baccalaureate degree yielded greater benefits for blacks than for their white counterparts. The need for cautious interpretation is similarly evident in the results on a variety of subsidiary issues, such as comparative life styles, that are treated in this volume. This book furnishes eloquent testimony that the recognition of complexity is the beginning of wisdom.

We could not conceal our admiration for *The Unequal Elites* even if this was our intention. But we do not pretend that we are neutral observers. Both authors were valued colleagues and we were present at the conception of this enterprise and shared the excitement of its maturity. Sydney Spivack would surely have taken satisfaction from Robert Althauser's craftsmanship. He would just as surely have been saddened by the persistence of racial inequality even among those whose educational careers were roughly comparable. But he would have been somewhat consoled by the recognition that black college graduates have had educational experiences that are their own excuse for being, and that nothing in *The Unequal Elites* need cause us to abandon the conviction that equal access to higher education for black people is at least a necessary, if insufficient, condition for racial equality.

MARVIN BRESSLER
MELVIN TUMIN

Princeton University

PREFACE

If I recall correctly, Sydney Spivack once told me that this study began with an idea of the distinguished black educator, Horace Mann Bond. Bond believed that the best way to study the effects of education received at a predominantly black school was to compare black and white classmates from integrated schools, with similar backgrounds and grades, and then to extend that comparison to similar blacks from predominantly black schools. Very much attracted to this idea, Spiv undertook such a study and secured its funding.

I became associated with the project early in 1967. My immediate task was to complete the first draft of the interview schedule; more generally, I was to construct a workable matched sample, as required by the study. Spiv shepherded the study through the period of data collection and early analysis until his untimely death in August 1969. Had he lived a year longer, this book (begun in February of 1970) would have been much the richer for his contribution to the analysis and his understanding of the findings. Lacking his assistance at this point, I take full responsibility for the specific content of this work and for any errors in it.

The project benefited from the financial support of several foundations, and the time, effort, and emotions of a great many people. The College Entrance Examination Board provided partial support for this study, as did the Ford,

Carnegie, Esso Education, Alfred P. Sloan, New York, Woodrow Wilson National Fellowship, Seth Sprague Education, John Hay Whitney, Field, and Roger Williams Straus Memorial foundations. The Princeton University Computer Center provided considerable computing time and Indiana University's Institute of Social Research provided typing facilities.

Marty Friendly, Linda Merrill, Hedy Straus, David Osterman, Lou Hendrix and Ann McGready carried out the early clerical work, compiling grade-point averages and father's occupations from college records, and doing literature reviews and coding. Several persons, including some in Princeton and Indiana University's sociology departments, assisted in typing the manuscript. I especially want to thank Louise Sparks, Florence Armstrong, Lois Long, Carol Schmiedeskamp, Kathleen Carpenter, Debbie Adams, Donna Hancock, and Wendy Allen.

The New York staff members of the National Opinion Research Center (NORC), which supervised the data collection and helped us design the interview schedule, were outstanding. I remember especially the patient help of Pearl Zinner and Roz Weisinger. We were also blessed with the programming, collaborative, and administrative skills of several able research assistants: Kay Kazarow, Beverly Amsel, John Balkcom, Michael Wigler, and Connie Chapman.

Colleagues who were kind enough to read and criticize earlier drafts of this book included Charles Bidwell, Marvin Bressler, Charles Glock, Everett Hughes, Elton Jackson, Donald Light, and Melvin Tumin. I am grateful for the time and thoughtful responses that help to sustain rich, collegial relationships.

Special thanks are due to eight people who made essential contributions to the completion of this work. As Spiv's wife and as his widow, Dorothy Spivack has been as generous and understanding as any project collaborator could wish. Joan Maruhnick, a secretary to the sociology department when I arrived at Princeton, provided both friendship and helpful advice during my early days at Princeton. Beverly Amsel was an able and gracious research associate during the two crucial years surrounding the interviewing, matching of respondents, and early data analysis. In recognition of her vital role in this study, Spiv and I have listed her as a collaborative author. I especially enjoyed the competent collaboration and original contributions of Michael Wigler, now a medical student at Columbia, and Donald Rubin of Educational Testing Service. Both were my coauthors on the three methodological papers that preceded this book. Wendy Allen did a superb job of editing grammar and correcting typographical errors in the penultimate draft of the manuscript.

Carolyn J. Mullins reorganized and copy edited the final draft of the manuscript, thereby making it more readable for educated laymen—something Spiv and I had wanted all along. For succor and faith throughout the difficult times in the last three years of work on this book, I am greatly indebted to Linda Hunkins.

None of this would have been possible without the cooperation of the college graduates who participated in this study. We offer these men our gratitude. To the blacks, in addition, we offer our awareness that their participation in studies typically conducted by whites is a gift of good will that must not be taken for granted. Should this work prompt some of the criticism and concern that well-known recent books on this topic have drawn, I trust I can respond with increased self-awareness and the same good will.

ROBERT P. ALTHAUSER

Bloomington, Indiana
September 1974

CONTENTS

TABLES AND FIGURES

TABLES

1

FIGURES

THE
UNEQUAL ELITES —————————

1

INTRODUCTION_____

It may be said that there is no harm in the fact that the Commission takes the economic system for granted and tries to see what can be done to overcome the handicaps which it causes by direct assistance to students and institutions. . . . The reply is that the Commission gives its powerful support to the omnibus fallacy, the doctrine that education, more education, more expensive education, will solve every problem and answer every prayer. The omnibus fallacy diverts the public mind from direct attack on the evil under consideration by proposing the easy, if costly, alternative, "let education do it!"

ROBERT M. HUTCHINS, on the *Report of the President's Commission on Higher Education, 1947* (Hofstadter and Smith, 1961:995–996).

D iscrimination has occurred when two or more groups of persons possess equal resources but are unequally rewarded. Years of schooling and of experience in the labor force, family background, and occupational status, among other factors, can be considered as resources; personal income, family income, and the status of occupations, as rewards. These definitions permit us to ask a very specific question about discrimination: Do black and white men find that their resources, when equal, produce rewards of equal value in the marketplace of human competition?

Education is the resource most often designated as paramount to achieving success and, not incidentally, to mitigating racial discrimination.

As contemporary controversies over busing, school funding, and environment versus heredity show, many social groups believe passionately in the benefits of schooling. Even proponents of conflicting uses of education share a common belief that *education makes a difference*, and thus is worth personal and collective investment. It is not surprising, then, that the fondest dream of many American parents who could not attend college has been that their children receive a college education. For black parents in particular, their children's college graduation must seem the key to a better life and to a living standard like that of similarly educated whites. At the very best, attainment of a college degree has been seen as guaranteeing blacks of the smallest possible economic handicap in a society that discriminates against blacks.

But does it? How well can a society use higher education to engender the success or personal growth of individuals, and to achieve such collective goals as the reduction or elimination of discrimination at the same time? To put both questions into a broader context, how likely is equalizing any one valued resource, such as education, or equalizing all major resources—that is, creating "equal opportunity"—to bring about equal rewards? If we focus on individual success and individual inequality, as Jencks (1972) does, the answer is apparently discouraging. Despite demands for equal results, and not merely equal opportunity, there is little agreement that equal results for individuals are either attainable or even generally desirable, much less the responsibility of governments to provide. More to the point, however, is the fact that arguments over the general effectiveness of education in reducing discrimination cannot be resolved by studying individual inequality.

A more appropriate focus—the one chosen for this research—is the success of individuals, or the equality of their rewards, *as members of competitive groups*. One can certainly argue, with Jencks, that the inequality of groups pales when compared with the magnitude of the inequality of individuals. However, one can argue equally cogently that the considerable and more visible inequality between, say, individuals in the top fifth versus the bottom fifth of the socioeconomic ladder accents the sociological and symbolic significance of group inequality. Racial groups' inequality may assume even greater importance sociologically when average differences between such groups are quantitatively smaller than those between individuals at the top and bottom.

The key question, then, is: To what extent can equal opportunity between groups yield equal results for those groups and, hence, the reduction of discrimination? Exploring this question requires defining "equal opportunity." Meanings such as "equal resources" or "entry into the job market on an equal footing" (Milner, 1972:24) are mere starting points, for then we must define an equal start. One possibility is to require equality in each resource shown to be highly related to success in any or all groups of individuals. Another possibility is average, overall equality, achieved through a "trade off" between individual resources—for example, unequal school resources could be used to counteract unequal family backgrounds. Groups characterized by such trade offs would be difficult to find. The first possibility is more attractive for its precision, but also hard to work with. Where do we find individuals for whom such equality holds? And what groups of people could be studied most advantageously?

Our research looked for the answer to both questions in groups of black and white college graduates of the same graduation years. If education is indeed a credible agent for reducing discrimination, it should, at minimum, have the same absolute effect on rewards such as income for members of both races. Furthermore, one would hope that the gap in black and white incomes and job statuses would decline as blacks and whites ascended the schooling ladder; that is, rewards would be equalized for the educational elites, the college graduates, of both groups. Unfortunately, past research into the postcollege achievements of black and white graduates indicates that obtaining higher education does not minimize or close the gap. In fact, the gap widens: Education does *not* have the same absolute effect on blacks' income as on whites'. To state this fact in terms we use throughout this book, education has less *income value* for blacks than for whites. College graduates bear the brunt of this inequality, and insofar as an educational elite symbolizes its group's potential for later achievement and reward, it is a crucial subject for the study of discrimination.

Simply comparing black and white graduates' incomes is obviously a crude approach, because college graduation per se in no way indicates the achievement of equal opportunity. Such equality entails multiple resources regardless of which of the above criteria we choose. We must therefore select groups of black and white graduates with as many equivalent starting points as is practicable. Certainly one such starting point should be education. We cannot use nominal years of education completed as a measure of educational equality because the average quality of education received at black or predominantly black colleges is inferior when compared with that received at white or integrated schools (Rose, 1944:288; Ginsberg, 1956; Broom and Glenn, 1965:90f; Jencks and Riesman, 1968:428–430).

Obviously, then, a valid test of the effects of increasing blacks' educational attainments should compare the postcollege achievements of white and black graduates of the *same* school, or at least of institutions offering education of comparable quality. Furthermore, some would argue that as a group, blacks entering these colleges are not as well prepared as whites. The former usually come from poorer families whose heads of households work at less prestigious jobs than the heads of their white classmates' families; as a partial result, blacks may earn poorer grade-point averages while in college.

So an even better comparison would result from matching black and white classmates (or at least graduates in the same year) (1) from institutions offering education of comparable quality, (2) with roughly the same grade-point average, and (3) from families of the same social class. Using these criteria, we selected more than 800 male black and white college alumni who had graduated between 1931 and 1964 from two integrated universities and one predominantly black university. This book examines the personal and family incomes, graduate education, jobs, and leisure-time activities of these men. Many of our analyses focus on the gap in average incomes between black and white graduates and on the relationship between personal income and four resources: education beyond the bachelor's degree, job status, years of experience since college graduation, and private-versus public-sector employment. Years of experience and employment sector have been largely neglected by sociologists, though economists routinely consider the former in their analyses.

We do not present a single analysis of all groups of graduates combined, nor are the white and the black groups analyzed separately. Rather, the analyses of income, job status, and other variables were done for subgroups of white and black graduates, for two reasons. First, although we matched our respondents for college education, grade-point average, years of experience, and father's job status (see Appendix A), the graduates from the different schools and racial groups had different backgrounds in other respects (see Chapter 3). Second, we had no theoretical or other a priori reason to expect that the income values of various resources for graduates from different schools would be the same. We further divided the six groups of graduates into those with and without graduate degrees, and those with public-versus private-sector employment. We did so expecting these resources to have quite different income values for the graduates in each group.

Our analyses use regression techniques that assume linear effects of resources on rewards.[1] Our findings are of three types. First, we estimate the absolute effects of resources on rewards, for example, the income or job-status value of years of experience since graduation. Second, we estimate the relative effects of different resources, for example, education and experience, on such rewards as job status. Finally, we decompose the differences in average incomes of black and white graduates into three components. *Component A* expresses the contribution to the overall difference of differences in the average level of resources; *component B*, of differences in the income values of these resources; and *component C*, of differences in the income value of other, unanalyzed variables describing blacks and whites, including the difference in racial group membership. The decompositions utilize a regression standardization technique. Such techniques have been little used by prior researchers working on this topic. Our particular technique is described in Althauser and Wigler (1972). Accompanying each analysis is a substantive interpretation of the statistics produced. The analyses of absolute and relative effects are sometimes interpreted together.[2] We have emphasized the different stories told by estimates of absolute and relative effects, paying greater attention to the former through their role in the decompositions. The result is distinctly less emphasis on the kinds of statistical results (e.g., explained variance; the size of path coefficients estimating relative effects) that have marked prior work on our topic.

To facilitate the cumulation of research findings, Chapter 2 reviews the results of past research most relevant to ours. Most of this literature does not concentrate on college graduates and thus does not indicate whether education has greater income value for white graduates or for black. A few studies have collected data on nationally representative subsamples of black college graduates. Unfortunately, such sampling yields too few black graduates to compare with the white. To increase the proportion of blacks in such samples, extra samples ("oversamples") of blacks are needed but have been drawn only in the most recent national studies, and these have not been confined to college graduates. The research reported in this book, confined to college graduates, compare with the white. To increase the proportion of blacks in such samples, covers a range of cohorts.

Chapter 3 briefly discusses the data and samples used in this research and then describes graduates' origins, backgrounds, graduate education, jobs, and incomes. Chapter 4 analyzes the income value of such resources as graduate education, years of experience, employment sector, and the status of graduates' jobs, and the status value (effect on status) of the first three of these resources. Both the absolute and the relative effects of these resources are estimated. The gap between average black and white incomes is then decomposed and discussed. Chapter 5, based largely on data for married graduates, considers the effect of income-producing resources on whether the graduates' wives work and examines the relative contributions of working wives and graduates to family incomes. Chapter 6 explores the leisure-time activities of graduates and the effects of color, income, graduate education, and other factors on these activities. We also examine data on graduates' actual (versus preferred) housing locations.

Chapter 7 summarizes and discusses findings of this research, together with their possible explanations and implications. Chapter 8 reflects on other implications and suggests directions for future research. That chapter concludes with a review of the descriptive, theoretical, and policy-making deficiencies of the literature on status attainment, of which this research is a part. The four appendixes cover methodological matters specific to our use of matched sampling, Duncan's socioeconomic index, significance tests, and regression standardization techniques to decompose the differences between black and white graduates' average personal incomes.

NOTES

1. Possible curvilinear effects were investigated; the generally unproductive results justify the linear assumptions made.

2. Measures of relative effects are often incorrectly compared across different groups or samples. Our interpretations avoid that error.

2

EQUALITY AND EDUCATION: PREVIOUS RESEARCH_____

P ast research has addressed three major topics: the income gap, the occupation gap, and college education as human capital. Reviewing this research is important for several reasons. First, it provides a context that permits us to determine the meaning and significance of findings. Second, it indicates the kinds of data and statistical results utilized in our study. Third, past findings should be closely compared and contrasted with our own results. Finally, some previous findings highlight the strategic importance of data on college graduates for understanding the discrimination generally encountered by blacks in the marketplace.

THE INCOME GAP

ABSOLUTE EFFECTS AND DECOMPOSITIONS

Table 2.1 shows the median incomes (in 1969 dollars) of whites and blacks, in 1949, 1959, and 1969, according to their years of education. The median income differences and ratios of nonwhite (black) to white (or total population) incomes are also shown. Two basic trends are worth noting. First, the general progression of increasing median differences and generally declining income ratios from lower to higher levels of education in all three time periods suggest the existence of negative incentives to complete additional education. This

TABLE 2.1 MEDIAN INCOMES OF WHITE AND BLACK MEN 25 YEARS OF AGE AND OLDER, IN 1949, 1959, AND 1969 (IN 1969 DOLLARS), BY EDUCATION AND RACE

Education[d] (years)	1949[a]				1959[b]				1969[c]			
	"White" (All)[e] (1)	Non-white (2)	(1) − (2) (3)	(2)/(1) (4)	White (5)	Non-white (6)	(5) − (6) (7)	(6)/(5) (8)	White (9)	Black (10)	(9) − (10) (11)	(10)/(9) (12)
Elementary school (<8)												
0	1706	1204	502	.70								
1–4	2102	1588	514	.76	3422	2300	1122	.67	3,613	2973	640	.82
5–7	3134	2293	841	.73	5031	3667	1364	.73	5,460	4293	1167	.79
8	3901	2851	1050	.73								
High school												
1–3	4492	3052	1440	.68	6313	4120	2193	.65	7,309	5222	2087	.71
4	5059	3457	1602	.68	6972	4713	2259	.68	8,613	6144	2487	.71
College												
1–3	5424	3473	1951	.64	7682	5089	2593	.66	9,575	7051	2524	.74
4+	6787	4055	2732	.60	9791	6150	3641	.62	12,437	8567	3870	.69

[a] *Source.* U.S. Bureau of the Census: U.S. Census of Population (1950: IV, Special Reports, Part 5, Chapter b, Table 13).
[b] *Source.* U.S. Bureau of the Census: U.S. Census of Population (1960: PC[1]-1D, 590; and PC[2]-5B, Table 6).
[c] *Source.* U.S. Bureau of the Census, 1969: Table 4.
[d] Measured by years of schooling.
[e] In 1959 data for Caucasians per se were not available; nor were data for blacks, as opposed to nonwhites generally, in 1949 and 1959. Hence "white" data in 1949 are actually data for the entire population, and the nonwhite data in 1949 and 1959 include Chinese, other nonwhites, and blacks.

trend indicates that blacks who have completed four years of college received smaller increments of increased income relative to their white counterparts than did blacks with lesser education. Second, for each level of education there is a general trend, over time, toward slightly higher ratios of black to white median incomes, but in general this fairly crude evidence indicates that black and white incomes are approaching parity only among the less educated; despite increases, during the last 10 years, in ratios for the better educated, we will have to see evidence that median income differences are dropping before we can expect any future income parity for the better educated.

Of course, these median differences do not control for the effects of other factors (e.g., years of experience, occupation, and geographic region). They are merely averages calculated across all possible categories of years of experience, region, and so forth. More sophisticated analyses consider the effect on income of variables other than education. For example, if black and white men in general and college graduates in particular have similar characteristics, do they derive similar incomes from jobs of comparable status? That is, does the possession of equal income-producing resources (e.g., comparable years of work experience) have equal value for both groups? Finally, what happens to the overall difference in mean or median incomes of black and white college graduates when these other factors are taken into account?

Few studies answer these questions. Few are devoted entirely or largely to college graduates, and few of these discuss black graduates as a distinguishable subgroup (although see, e.g., Reed and Miller, 1970). However, several analyses of more general data include adequate samples of black men, college graduates among them, and provide us with some relevant findings. Some of these studies have estimated that the mean income difference between black and white college graduates, favoring whites, widens with additional years of experience. According to Thurow's (1967) analysis of 1960 Census data, the income gap for male college graduates with 20 years of experience was $1900 greater than the gap for men with 5 years of experience. Similarly, Blum and Coleman (1970:54) found that the income gap grew from $1000 for black and white male college graduates aged 30 to $2000 at age 34, to $3000 at age 38.

Other studies show that a sizable income gap still remains when other factors not directly associated with discrimination are controlled. Such gaps imply a considerable effect of skin color on earnings, especially for college graduates. Thus, in one study, a $4566 income gap for college graduates was reduced by a mere 17 percent (to $3800) when occupational distribution and region of residence were controlled; this figure is the smallest percentage reduction in the mean income gap for men at any level of education (Siegel, 1965; findings based on 1960 Census data). Working with 1967 data on college graduates, 5 percent of whom were nonwhites, Reed and Miller (1970) reduced a gap ranging from $3300 to $4250 to about $2400 by controlling for college rank[1] and job choice ("field of specialization"). However, the authors point out that the remaining gap can be considered a conservative estimate of the effect of color on earnings, since the 5 percent sample included small numbers of Japanese- and Chinese-Americans as well as blacks. They also point out that roughly 34 percent of the reduction reflects blacks' "choice" (our quotes) of lower-paying specialties, such as teaching, and the larger proportion of blacks, in contrast to whites, that attended lower-ranked colleges.

Other regression analyses of income and income-producing factors, using national samples *not* confined to college graduates, have found that the income value of occupational status is considerably greater for white than for black men, even when such factors as education and family background are simultaneously controlled (Duncan, 1969).[2] Furthermore, the income value of education is much greater for white than black men (Duncan, 1969; Blum, 1972:282),[3] even when a host of other background and intervening factors are taken into account.[4] The income value of father's occupational status is greater for whites than blacks, when father's educational level is controlled (Duncan, 1969).[5] However, the income value of father's education is greater for black than for white men, when father's occupational status (Duncan, 1969) or prestige (Blum, 1972:276) is controlled.[6] To summarize, then, the incomes of white men generally benefit more from the possession of additional amounts of most income-producing resources than do the incomes of black men. Overall, blacks' and whites' incomes diverge from each other as resources increase. The situation resembles that shown in Figure 2.1.

Figure 2.1 has three important features. First, the circles on the top and bottom lines represent the mean income and mean resources of each group; the white male's average income and average resources clearly exceed the black's. Second, the slope of the line for whites is steeper than that for blacks; the difference indicates the greater income value of various resources for whites. Third, across the entire range of resources, white men's incomes always exceed blacks'.

This picture apparently holds true generally, even when we consider the income value of one resource within categories of another. Siegel, for example, plotted the relationship between mean income and years of schooling completed within the major occupational (Census) categories: professionals, technical (and related) workers; managers, officials, and proprietors; clerical;

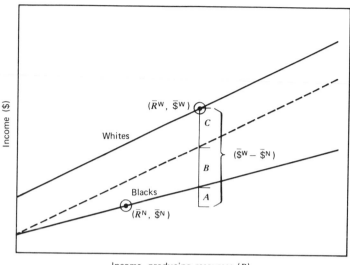

Figure 2.1   Decomposing mean black and white personal income differences $(\bar{\$}^W - \bar{\$}^N)$ into A, B, and C components.

sales; and so on. Differences in mean income between whites and blacks almost always increased with additional years of education (Siegel, 1965:52).

With the three features in mind, we can ask some interesting, policy-relevant questions raised by previous regression analyses of income. First, how much of the gap in average incomes between whites and blacks is due to blacks' having fewer average resources? Second, how much is due to the lower income values of the resources that blacks possess? Third, how much is unexplained by the first two differences and due, in part, to skin color? Answering these questions requires decomposing the average income difference into the three components that are implied by the question. A represents the difference between whites and blacks in the average level of one or more income-producing resources possessed. B represents the difference in slopes (income values) of blacks' and whites' resources. C represents the effects of other factors not explicitly included in the A and B *components;* prominent among those factors, we presume, is color.[7] This technique—regression standardization—is actually quite simple in principle, but the approach just described (used throughout this work and detailed originally in Althauser and Wigler, 1972) differs from that used by Blum (1972) and Duncan (1969) in their decompositions of mean income differences.[8]

If we reanalyze Blum's and Duncan's data following our decomposition procedure, the results can be represented by graphs like Figure 2.1, or indeed, as it turns out, by Figure 2.1 itself. The largest component of the three, according to both data sets, is the *B component;* that is, more of the income gap is accounted for by the greater income value of white men's resources than by either of the other two components. In particular, differences in average resources between whites and blacks (e.g., the higher average of whites' educational level or occupational prestige) contribute considerably less to the income gap than does the greater responsiveness of whites' incomes to the actual resources possessed.[9]

The implications of the latter result are quite important both for our understanding of discrimination and inequality and for policy. If the present income gap is not primarily due to blacks' having less education, lower job status, or fewer income-producing resources on the average than whites, then it is unlikely that merely increasing the average amount of blacks' resources through job training, for example, or raising the proportion of black men with higher-status jobs and college degrees, would produce equal mean incomes. Rather, the results loosely suggest that the *income value of resources must be equalized in order to achieve overall equality of incomes.* Clearly, the whole structure of individual resources and rewards needs to be carefully examined and evaluated.

Given that college graduates have above-average levels of education and job status when compared with men generally, the foregoing suggests a larger-than-average gap in incomes among college graduates. However, the more interesting question—one that we examine in our data—is: Does the income value of these resources diverge as graduates increase (1) their level of education by completing graduate degrees, (2) their job status, or (3) their years of experience?

RELATIVE EFFECTS

A different set of questions focuses on the relative effects of different resources on the incomes of black and white men. Are there differences between blacks and whites in the degree to which different resources produce income? If so, do the available data suggest that the use made of different resources by the labor market is different for black than for white men?

There are many ways to measure relative effects;[10] the most common, though not necessarily the best for all purposes, involves comparing various path or standardized regression coefficients within groups of whites and blacks. Such coefficients are, in effect, measures of our ability to explain the variance in, or estimate, an individual's income from our knowledge of his resources (e.g., his particular educational level or years of experience). The focus is *not* on the relative size of corresponding coefficients (or the variance in income explained by education) for whites and blacks but on the contrasts, if any, between the rank order of different coefficients (or combinations of coefficients) *within* white and black groups.

Using path analysis, several sociologists (Duncan, 1969; Coleman et al., 1972) have found evidence that black and white men use education and job status differently to gain income. Their data are not strictly comparable (see note 3, this Chapter); nonetheless, there is a crude convergence in their findings. In essence it appears that more than black men, whites tend to use job status to gain their incomes (see Duncan, 1969; Coleman et al., 1972; and Blum, 1972). Black and white men also differ in their use of educational advantages. For both groups, education yields income both directly and indirectly, that is, by permitting acquisition of a job that brings income in proportion to its status (see Duncan, 1969). For whites, the indirect effect is greater than the direct effect; for blacks, the direct effect is stronger.

This finding is *not* that whites gain more income from a unit increment of education by indirect than by direct means, or that blacks gain more income from a unit increment of education by direct than by indirect means. The finding refers only to the *relative* degree to which income is directly or indirectly determined by education. However, insofar as it affects income directly and indirectly, whites gain *absolutely* more income from each unit increment of education. Given this difference in the absolute degree to which the two groups convert education into income by either route, the incomes of both groups are relatively, but differently, determined by education.

Coleman et al. (1972) and Blum (1972) reach virtually the same conclusions, using different lists of income-producing resources and, in part, different techniques. Whether because of different tastes, such as a preference for income over job status, or because of different labor market processes, such as in matching jobs to qualified men, whites apparently "choose" status over income, expecting the former to yield later income; blacks, in contrast, apparently "choose" initial income, expecting it to yield increased job status and appropriate income at a later time. Whites enjoy modest success with their approach; blacks do not.

These findings posed a simple question for our research: Are the same patterns evident among our college graduates?

THE OCCUPATION GAP

Another question should also be investigated. Have prior researchers found differences in the jobs of black and white men, controlling for their educational levels? Differences in occupational status were investigated by Blau and Duncan (1967:208).[11] After controlling for father's job status and respondent's first-job status, they found that the gap in average job status grew from 6 points (among American-born men with less than 9 years of education) to 8.8 and then 12.2 points (for men with 1 to 3 and 4 years of high school, respectively); the figure then dropped somewhat to 10.4 for men with some education at college level or above. However, this modest move toward equal status among college matriculants and graduates does not substantially alter the essentially increasing inequality in average occupational status (similar to the increasing inequality of median income noted above) as men complete additional education.

Differences in the distribution of black and white men into Census occupational categories seem to tell a different story (see Hare, 1965:172; Broom and Glenn, 1965:125). These authors use an "index of dissimilarity" to measure differences in the distribution of proportions of black and white men into each category. This index is the proportions of blacks (or of whites, for that matter) in various occupational categories that would have to be redistributed in order for the proportions of blacks and whites in each category to be identical.[12] These researchers found that when age and cohort are controlled, occupational dissimilarity (in 1940, 1950, and 1960) increased directly with educational attainment until men had completed 4 years of high school. Occupations then became more similar (equally distributed) among men with 1 to 3 years of college, and were most similar for men with 4 years of college!

Combining these two sets of findings with those on income indicates that for college graduates, most of all, there is considerable racial inequality, in terms of both job status and income, *within* broad occupational categories. Thus Broom and Glenn (1965:112) remind us that within many of the major occupational groups, blacks are concentrated in jobs with less prestige and lower pay. The number of black professionals may have increased over the last 30 years, but they have been concentrated, for example, in "relatively low-paying semiprofessional occupations, such as welfare and recreation workers, medical and dental technicians" (Broom and Glenn, 1965:112). These kinds of differences are not immediately apparent in either Hare's or Broom and Glenn's data, but they help to account for the gaps in average income and job status noted earlier. They also make black and white college graduates particularly interesting to study.

COLLEGE EDUCATION AS HUMAN CAPITAL

The acquisition of income-producing resources can be analyzed as an investment having various rates of return. Economists taking this "human capital" approach to education have estimated the return to private individuals (and to society) of completing various amounts of schooling. For example, according to one definition (Hines et al., 1970), the private rate of return to education is the rate of interest one would pay to finance some amount of education and still break even afterward, when education is put to use in the marketplace. These rates of return take into account the costs of schooling, such as tuition, books, and travel, and "opportunity costs," such as income foregone during the period of school attendance. The foregone income for college graduates, for example, would be the median income of high-school graduates aged 18 to 21 (see Schultz, 1960). This rate is then variously compared with the return from such alternative forms of investments as savings accounts (4 to 5 percent) or common stocks (10 percent after taxes), and so forth. These rates do not consider nonpecuniary returns or consumption benefits, and their estimates can be biased by failure to control for the effects of ability, discrimination, unemployment, and other factors.

Many studies have estimated the rate of return to a college or a postgraduate education (Hansen, 1963; Becker, 1964; Hanoch, 1967; Rogers, 1969; Hines et al., 1970; Taubman and Wales, 1973). Not totally comparative, these estimates vary considerably (from 0 to 30 percent), as do the conclusions drawn about the viability of investments in education. For example, Taubman and Wales found that college dropouts enjoyed higher rates of return than college graduates! Becker and Hansen found the opposite.

Very few studies have compared the private returns of blacks and whites. One that did (Hines et al., 1970) estimates the returns from completing college for nonwhite men at 6 percent; for white men, 14 percent. The rates for nonwhite women (20 percent) surpassed those for white women (9 percent) and for both groups of men. The authors note, however, that discrimination reduces the rates of return from alternative investments by blacks, thus modestly improving the objective attractiveness of college for black men. Hines et al. did not control for labor force participation rates. However, estimates from this and other studies (Mincer, 1962; Becker, 1964; Hanoch, 1967) agree that rates of return to black men for completing college are less than those to white men.

In our study we did not estimate rates of return from postgraduate education because we lacked data regarding graduates' foregone income (i.e., data on incomes of black and white high-school graduates whose backgrounds and abilities were comparable to those of our college graduates, and to each others'). Nonetheless, the unknown rates of return are proportional to the income value of at least some of our college graduates' educations to a greater extent than would be true if a random sample of black and white college graduates had been studied. We know that the black and white classmates in our samples experienced roughly the same costs of undergraduate schooling. If we take grade-point averages as a suitable measure of ability, these matched black and white graduates should also have been similarly able. Given this much similarity, the unknown costs of graduate education and the unknown foregone earnings during college and postgraduate years may also be fairly similar, although we cannot be sure.[13]

To summarize, then, much previous work has been broadly concerned with the social and economic inequality of whites and blacks. Researchers have found that substantial gaps in median and average incomes and in job status separate white and black men; furthermore, these gaps are generally wider for college men than for those with less education. The income gap for college graduates remains substantial even after statistical adjustments have been made to control for the influence of such factors as age, college rank, and geographic region. Moreover, the income value of several income-producing resources is distinctly less for black than for white men in general. In fact, after decomposing this income gap, we found that the *B component*—reflecting the income values of various resources—was larger than the *A component*, which reflects differences in the average level of blacks' and whites' resources. Furthermore, black and white men use such resources as education and job status to produce income in different ways. Finally, the rate of return to a college education for black men has been estimated to be less than that for white men.

In short, the literature that has dealt specifically with education suggests that at least in the past, completing increasing amounts of education has not provided clearly effective relief from economic inequality. If anything, the acquisition of additional education has been associated with the maintenance of, or even an increase in, the inequality of black and white men. This situation flatly contradicts popular notions about the role of education in American society and its effectiveness in neutralizing racial discrimination.

NOTES

1. The authors also underscore the importance of college rank in their finding that going to a better school provides more of an advantage for those with postgraduate degrees. Though other studies discuss the importance of college rank (Welch, 1966; Sharp, 1970; Taubman and Wales, 1973) as well as class rank (Wiesbrod and Karpoff, 1968), none refers specifically to black graduates.

2. Duncan (1969) found that 10 units of occupational status corresponded to $200 of additional income for black men, and $700 for white men. These estimates controlled for number of siblings and the education and occupational status of the head of the household in which the male respondents were raised.

3. The Duncan (1969) and Blum (1972) data are not strictly comparable, though both came from national samples; Blum and her associates added a supplementary sample of black males. The notable differences are these: Duncan worked from a national survey of 20,700 men, aged 20 to 64, in the civilian, noninstitutional population of the United States, as of March, 1962. Coleman and Blum worked from a national sample of 1589 men aged 30 to 39 as of 1968. Their analysis of blacks and whites, covering a full 10 years of occupational experience, was based on a sample of 1254 men, 47 percent of whom were black. Thus Coleman and Blum's data are confined to one cohort of men, while Duncan's cover several. Though Coleman and Blum control many more factors than Duncan—including 14 that describe residential movement, occupational activity, marital and family characteristics, and educational attainments between the first job (after completing full-time schooling) and the "later" job (10 years after the first job)—they never relate income to job status for the same period, early or late. Hence we cannot compare their data and Duncan's with respect to the relative sizes of (1) the direct effect of education on income and (2) education's indirect effect through job status. Finally, their job status measures are different: Duncan used his socioeconomic index; Coleman and Rossi used Siegel's measure of occupational prestige.

4. We estimate that in Duncan's analysis, an increment of two years of schooling corresponds to an additional $343 and $596 of annual income for black and white men, respectively; in Coleman and Blum's data, to $331 and $698, respectively. These estimates are based on several assumptions made partly to overcome the difficulties posed by the incomparability of the two analyses. First, we ignored the effects of differences between Duncan's and Siegel's measures of job status (the latter, of course, used by Coleman and Blum). Second, we ignored the fact that Coleman and Blum's income data are for a date 10 years after schooling was completed, while Duncan's are personal income at the time of the survey (thus the income data are for men at different stages of their careers). Third, we disregarded the fact that Coleman and Blum controlled many more variables than did Duncan. Two other differences were *not* ignored: the different coding of completed schooling; and the fact that Duncan includes, while Coleman and Blum exclude, the effect of current-job status on current income. Coleman and Blum coded education on a scale ranging from 0 to 8, the scale values corresponding to such categories as: less than 4 years of schooling, 4 to 7 years, 8 years, and so on, to 4 years of college, and 5 or more years of college. As a rough approximation, we equated a difference of 2 years of schooling in Duncan's data with a difference of one unit on Coleman and Blum's educational scale. To make Duncan's partial regression of in-

come on schooling more comparable to Coleman and Blum's, we added the indirect effect of schooling on income through job status to schooling's direct effect on income.

5.   For black men, Duncan found no significant relationship between the job status of the head of the respondent's household and the respondent's income; 10 units of status corresponded to $200 additional income for white men. Blum found no significant relationship for either blacks or whites.

6.   In Duncan's analysis, we find that insofar as father's completed schooling affected son's schooling (and through son's schooling, son's income), two years of schooling completed by the respondent's father (or head of household) corresponds to $81 of added income for blacks and $68 for whites. In neither Duncan's nor Blum's analysis is the direct effect of father's education on income significant. Disregarding statistical significance for the moment, Blum's analysis supports Duncan's finding that father's (or head of household's) education has more income value for blacks than for whites.

7.   The graphic counterparts of these components are shown in Figure 2.1. If the average level of blacks' resources equaled the average level of whites', while the income value of blacks' resources remained as it was, an *A component's* worth of the mean income difference could be statistically eliminated. If we next made the slope of the blacks' line equal to that for whites (i.e., if, by statistical manipulation, we assigned to blacks the income value of resources enjoyed by whites), we could account for a *B component's* worth of the income gap. Finally, if we were to assign black men the same income as whites with identical resources (i.e., made the blacks' and whites' lines coincide), we would eliminate a *C component's* worth of the gap. It should be noted that components can be negative—blacks' average resources may *exceed* whites', or the income values of blacks' resources may exceed whites', or the incomes corresponding to identical resources may be greater for blacks than for whites.

8.   Any approach to regression standardization requires that the values of each resource be referred to meaningful zero points. Our approach differs from other methods by defining this point near the lower end of the range of values for each resource. For example, 16 rather than zero is a meaningful zero point for "years of education among a sample of college graduates."

9.   This result is consistent with Duncan's findings, but not Blum's. The difference results from the different formulas used by the two researchers.

10.   See Cain and Watts (1970). The decomposition of mean income differences above entailed a different measure of relative effects, namely, the product of a resource's unstandardized regression coefficient and the mean value of that resource.

11.   See Appendix B for a description of Duncan's socioeconomic index and its use in our research.

12.   For example, suppose there were only three occupational groups: executives, bricklayers, and handymen. Suppose further that in a group of blacks, 30 percent were executives, 30 percent were bricklayers, and 40 percent handymen, while in a white group, 50 percent were executives, 30 percent bricklayers, and 20 percent handymen. If we take the difference between whites and blacks for each of the three pairs of proportions, we obtain +20, 0, and −20 percent, respectively. The index used above is the sum of these differences, hence 0.20. The greater this value, the greater the dissimilarity of the occupational distributions of black and white men; many different sets of distributions would produce the same index value.

13.   Census data on 1960 incomes of men 18 to 24 years old with high-school degrees, living outside the South, show whites with higher median and mean incomes (e.g., medians were $3117 for whites, $2473 for blacks). These data indicate moderately higher foregone earnings for whites. Data for incomes of college graduates 18 to 24, relevant to earnings foregone while in graduate school, give similar indications.

3

GRADUATES' BACKGROUNDS, EDUCATION, JOBS, AND INCOME_____

E ducation was to constitute blacks' release from the social heritage of plantation life. Yet this heritage—the social background and characteristics commonly associated with being black—has both blocked their acquisition of education and been used to explain why educating blacks has failed to overcome white discrimination. Presumably black college graduates' social heritage provides fewer disadvantages in job competition than that of any other educational class of blacks. Nevertheless, all such characteristics should be considered possible explanations for the relative degrees of economic success attained by our college graduates. At the very least, there should be differences between white and black graduates with respect to some of these characteristics if they have indeed caused different success rates. This chapter first considers backgrounds. We then examine, for blacks and whites, the amount of graduate education they completed, their jobs, and their incomes.

DATA AND SAMPLES

We studied matched samples of black and white graduates from three universities. We named the two integrated schools Atlantic State University (ASU) and Metropolitan State University (MSU); we named the primarily

Negro school, Frazier University (after the late, distinguished black sociologist, E. Franklin Frazier). All three schools are located in the East, and most of the alumni that we contacted resided (at that time) in the East. Details on the selection, matching, and interviewing are included in Appendix A. At this point we will note only that we matched each pair of black and white graduates for year of graduation, grade-point average, and father's (or head of household's) job at the time the respondents attended college.[1] The interviews were conducted by the National Opinion Research Center (NORC).

We developed four matched comparisons of black and white graduates from our sample. White graduates from each integrated school are matched with their black classmates; mutually exclusive subsamples of Frazier graduates (here labeled Frazier–1 and Frazier–2) were also matched with ASU and MSU blacks but compared with ASU and MSU whites, respectively. Thus ASU whites are compared with ASU blacks and Frazier–1 blacks; and MSU whites, with MSU blacks and Frazier–2 blacks. Since the same white graduates are compared with two groups of black graduates each, the four comparisons are not totally independent of each other.

We can presume that the quality of education received by matched ASU and MSU classmates was virtually equal. Regarding the quality of education received by the white versus Frazier black graduates, the average of two measures of quality used in Astin's (1965) study (one reflecting common measures of scholastic aptitude and the other, a student body's level of ability)[2] were essentially identical for the three schools. Other schools of comparable quality, incidentally, included Fisk University and Ohio State University. Schools just below this level included Morehouse College and Howard University; the University of North Carolina at Chapel Hill was just above.

Using six subsamples in four matched comparisons complicated our presentation of the data. When preparing the tables, we often found that two of the subsamples had similar distributions on one or more characteristics. Therefore, in the interest of simplification, when this situation occurred, we combined the data for these characteristics (such combinations are centered between the columns involved).[3] Furthermore, information about each variable or characteristic for each and every graduate was not always obtained. However, the frequency and amount of such missing data were not sufficient to be worth noting in these tables.[4]

FAMILY BACKGROUNDS

Table 3.1 presents information on the graduates' backgrounds. The discussion of each variable is preceded by the line number of that variable in the table.

GRADUATES' ORIGINS AND FAMILIES' CHARACTERISTICS

1. Although the sampled schools were located in the northeastern United States, the well-known migration of blacks from the South to the North had obviously affected the black graduates' families: a much higher proportion of black than white graduates were *born* in the South. However, the size of the difference in these proportions is modest (ranging from 18 to 28 percent). Small proportions of the white and Frazier graduates were born abroad, but the vast majority of graduates (96 percent or more of each sample) were born in the United States.

2. When we considered whether a graduate's *home town* was a city, suburb, or small town,[5] we found differences according to school as well as race. Roughly three-fourths of MSU blacks, MSU whites, and Frazier graduates came from cities. In contrast, white ASU graduates came less frequently from the cities (50 percent) and more from the suburbs (14 percent) and small towns (30 percent). The black ASU graduates showed still another pattern: 66 percent were born in cities and only 20 percent in small towns. Despite these differences, the percentage differences between samples are modest (the maximum difference was 28 percent). At this point, then, the subsamples do not differ radically.

3. Our impressions change, however, when we consider *father's birthplace*. About half of our white graduates were sons of immigrants and, as such, the first generation born in this country. In an interesting parallel, we found a majority of the black graduates to be northern-born sons of southern-born fathers and, hence, the first generation of their families to be born in the North. The two white samples differ in one respect: while about half of the white graduates had fathers born in the United States, greater proportions of ASU graduates' foreign-born fathers came from northwestern Europe and various Commonwealth countries, while greater proportions of the MSU graduates' fathers came from Central and Eastern European countries. The ASU and MSU black samples were similar enough to be combined. This combined sample differed from the combined Frazier samples in that a larger proportion (9 percent) of the Frazier graduates' fathers were from the West

TABLE 3.1 ORIGINS AND SOCIAL CHARACTERISTICS OF GRADUATES

Origins and Social Characteristics	ASU Blacks[a]	MSU Blacks[a]	ASU Whites	MSU Whites	Frazier-1 Blacks	Frazier-2 Blacks
1. Birthplace[b] (%)						
South	19	29	1			26
North	80	71	95			71
Outside U.S.A.	1	0	4			3
2. Hometown (%)						
Urban	66	77	50	75		74
Suburban	13	4	14	11		4
Small town	20	16	30	12		21
3. Father's birthplace (%)						
Outside U.S.A.						
Northwestern Europe, Canada, Australia	0		12	7		0
Central and Eastern Europe	0		14	30		0
Southern Europe, Middle East, North Africa	1		17	15		0
West Indies	3		0	0		9
Inside U.S.A.						
South	73		1	1		62
North	23		54	47		26
4. Father's education (average)	9.5		8.4	8.0	9.8	10.7
% Grade school or less	24	24	24	37	21	15
% Some college or more	14	21	6	9	20	26
5. Mother's education (average)	10.1		9.3	8.3	10.6	11.1
% Grade school or less	21	18	14	31	12	13
% Some college or more	21	17	7	9	16	29

Variable						
6. Mothers employed full time (%)	66	72	75	84	57	62
7. Mother's job status (average)	23	20	38	31	28	33
8. Number of siblings (average)	3.0			1.9		2.8
9. From intact family (%)	75	64		85	75	66
10. Primary means of college financing (%)						
Parents	16	14	31	23	42	43
Working	28	21	25	25	10	16
G.I. Bill	26	43	32	32	10	16
Scholarships	25	16	10	18	19	19
Other (loans, relatives)	5	6	2	2	5	6
11. Religious preference (%)						
Protestant	75	84	25	30	68	85
Catholic	4	5	44	29	16	5
Jewish	1	0	16	34	0	0
None	18	10	11	4	15	9
12. Geographic residence in 1966 (%)						
New York, New Jersey, Pennsylvania	83	88	83	92		74
South, New England	4	2	3	2		6
Other	13	9	14	6		20
13. Type of residential area (%)						
Urban	65	81	20	37		77
Suburban	25	11	36	44		11
Small town	10	8	42	17		11
N	127	155	126	155	127	149

[a] Numbers centered between two columns are a combined figure for the two; in such cases the two figures were similar enough to make separation unnecessary.

[b] Variables are described in text.

Indies, while a larger (by 11 percent) proportion of ASU and MSU graduates had southern-born fathers.

4. The *father's amount of education* also differs. The white graduates' fathers completed an average of 8.0 and 8.4 years of education, while the Frazier graduates' fathers averaged two additional years. The fathers of the other black graduates fell between these two groups, though their average years of education completed was closer to that of Frazier than of ASU and MSU white graduates. If we examine the percentages of fathers completing certain rungs on the educational ladder, we find that the Frazier graduates' fathers more often completed at least some college and/or postcollege work than did the white or black ASU graduates' fathers. The modal level of education for all samples was "some high school."

5. The *mothers' average amount of education completed* was consistently higher (about 0.5 years more) than the fathers'. While the modal level was still "some high school," these women were less concentrated proportionately at the lowest level (grade school or less) than the fathers. Roughly the same statement can be made about the proportions who were college graduates or had done postcollege work. As was true of the fathers, the mothers of Frazier graduates completed more education, on the average, than did the mothers of the ASU and MSU graduates; furthermore, the mothers of white graduates completed less education than the mothers of all black graduates. The greater education of both fathers and mothers is particularly noteworthy when we recall that fathers' job statuses were largely equalized when the matched samples were created. The implication of this fact is that black fathers' education benefited them less in the job market than it did white fathers.

6 and 7. The same situation held for *mothers' employment*. Frazier graduates' mothers were more often employed[6] than were the mothers of ASU or MSU black graduates who, in turn, were employed more often than white mothers. However, the white mothers generally held higher-status jobs. In short, black mothers with higher average educational attainments worked more often and at jobs with lower average status than did white mothers.

8. We also gathered data on graduates' *number of brothers and sisters*. We might expect that black graduates came from larger families than white graduates, given the popularly assumed higher fertility of blacks. However, we are not dealing with white and black families in general but rather with those of college graduates. The data show that black graduates averaged three siblings each, or one more than white graduates. White graduates were more often only children or brothers of one to three siblings.

9.   Finally, we measured *family intactness*.[7] The popular notion is that "real" fathers or mothers are absent from black homes to a greater extent than white parents because of higher separation or divorce rates. Here we distinguished four categories. If both natural parents were with the graduate most of the time during which he grew to age 16, we categorized his family as intact. If the graduate had two adoptive parents, or one natural parent and one stepparent or adoptive parent, his family was defined as nearly intact. If he had one natural and one missing or absent parent, or two foster parents, his family was defined as more nonintact. Finally, if he was raised in an institution, or by male or female relatives or nonrelatives, he was categorized as coming from a nonintact family. An easy majority of graduates in all samples came from intact families. As expected, a higher proportion of whites than blacks did so: 81 to 87 percent of black graduates came from intact or nearly intact families, compared to 93 percent of the white graduates. However, the difference between the races was not as great as might have been expected.

OTHER VARIABLES

10.   Knowing that the black graduates tended to come from larger and slightly less intact families than did whites, we might expect that blacks more than whites had to work their way through college, receive scholarship aid, utilize the GI Bill, or use some combination of these *financial aids*.[8] In addition, blacks' parents had more education, but equivalent or lower-status jobs than whites. To summarize the findings briefly, ASU and MSU black graduates showed much greater reliance on means other than parental assistance. In contrast, Frazier graduates relied more on parental financing than any other group of graduates. They also worked their way through college and used the assistance of the GI Bill less than any other sample. White graduates used parental assistance less often than Frazier graduates but more often than ASU and MSU black graduates.

11.   We now consider three characteristics of graduates at the time our data were collected (1967–1968). Recalling the fairly large proportions of white graduates whose fathers were born abroad, we might well expect sizable proportions of non-Protestants among the white graduates. In contrast, blacks in general have been fairly heavily Protestant; we thus expected our black graduates to be largely Protestant. The data on *religious preference* support both expectations. Among the two white samples, about 60 percent are either Jewish or Catholic: many more from ASU are Catholic, while about the same

proportions—a third each—from MSU are Jewish and Catholic. All four black samples have Protestant majorities.

12.   In confining this study to graduates of colleges in the eastern region of the United States, we presumed that most of the graduates would settle in this same *geographic region* after college. From this presumption it followed that black and white graduates would have sought employment in the same occupational market, thus lessening possible variation in the opportunities for employment and advancement experienced by all graduates. Our data do not permit an unbiased estimate of the actual proportion of all graduates who did or did not settle in a particular region. Although we tried to locate graduates who had moved out of the Middle Atlantic States (New York, eastern Pennsylvania, and New Jersey) after college, the proportions in our sample living outside this area probably underestimate the actual proportions of all graduates from our schools and graduation years. However, it still seems clear that most of the graduates in each sample resided, and thus presumably worked, in this region. To a surprising extent, the largest percentage (20 percent) of any sample (Frazier blacks) to settle outside the Middle Atlantic area favored regions other than the South or New England. Our figures also suggest that MSU graduates probably remain in the Middle Atlantic area more often than ASU graduates.

13.   Although most of our graduates resided in the East, their *residential areas* were not necessarily similar. Our common-sense notion is that whites live outside the larger cities while blacks live within them, and indeed, our white graduates lived primarily in suburbs and small towns, while the blacks lived mostly in the cities. The MSU and Frazier black graduates were similarly located: 77 to 81 percent lived in the cities, and about 10 percent each in the suburbs and small towns. In contrast, ASU's black graduates had a large contingent (25 percent) living in the suburbs and about 15 percent less in the city than the other two black samples. MSU white graduates congregated in the suburbs and cities, largely avoiding small towns. ASU whites, in contrast, favored small towns and suburbs, largely avoiding the cities.

SUMMARY

On three characteristics (college financing, mother's full-time employment, and geographic region of present residence) we found no clear differences between the black and the white samples as a whole, even though there were often interesting differences between specific subsamples. On several other variables, modest percentage differences distinguished black and white graduates. Overall, the black graduates more often than the whites were born in the South and raised in urban home towns. The blacks also had more highly educated parents and more siblings, but they came from intact families less often than white graduates, and their mothers worked in lower-status jobs than did the whites' mothers. The data on father's birthplace, graduates' religious preferences, and rural-urban locale of present residence showed the strongest differences between black and white graduates. Black graduates' fathers were typically southern-born; about half of white graduates' fathers were born in the northern United States, and about half were foreign-born. Protestant affiliations were especially typical of black graduates, while whites were more evenly spread among Protestant, Catholic, and Jewish affiliations. Blacks lived predominantly in urban areas, while whites favored the suburbs and small towns.

EDUCATION, JOBS, AND INCOME

GRADUATE EDUCATION

Many of our sample members entered graduate school immediately following completion of undergraduate training. Some went to graduate school for one or more years without receiving degrees; others both attended and received degrees. We assigned different numbers, representing "years of school," for the various kinds of degrees received (for example, 2 for a Master's degree of any sort, 5 for a Ph.D., 6 for an M.D., 3 for an LL.B. or B.D.; see Table 3.2).[9]

1 and 2.   Somewhere between 31 and 48 percent of our graduates completed work for some *graduate or professional degree.* If we compare mean years of education for white and black college graduates, we find a startling result. *Black graduates within each of the four cohorts of matched samples completed more years of graduate education leading to degrees than did white graduates.* Differences of just over half a year of schooling characterize the two oldest groups of graduates; this figure narrows to roughly a quarter of a year for the two younger cohorts. The latter differences are not interpreted here because some graduates in these two cohorts may yet complete their graduate work. We therefore do not conclude that the mean differences are definitely narrowing among the younger graduates. However, it appears that more of the younger black graduates than white will complete graduate-degree work.

TABLE 3.2 EDUCATION, JOB CHARACTERISTICS, AND PERSONAL INCOME OF GRADUATES

Education, Job Characteristics, and Personal Income	ASU Blacks	MSU Blacks	ASU Whites	MSU Whites	Frazier-1 Blacks	Frazier-2 Blacks
1. With a graduate degree (%)	44	48	31	39	39	44
2. Years of graduate education[a] (overall mean)	1.3	1.3	0.9	1.0	1.2	1.8
Classes of 1931–1948 (mean)	1.4	2.2	0.9	1.6	2.6	2.5
Classes of 1949–1954 (mean)	1.6	1.3	1.0	1.1	1.8	2.1
Classes of 1955–1959 (mean)	1.9	1.2	1.6	0.9	0.8	1.6
Classes of 1960–1964 (mean)	0.6	0.8	0.4	0.7	0.4	1.4
3. Professions/business (%)						
Professionals and technical	72	74	58	70	82	
Managers, officials, proprietors	18	20	32	23	14	
4. In Public-sector jobs (%)	59	78	27	61	75	66
5. Employment sector (%)						
Private sector						
Self-employed	13	10	18	11	13	
Salaried	28	11	55	28	17	
Public sector						
Nonprofit	10	17	6	12	19	
Government	49	61	21	49	51	
6. Specific jobs (%)						
M.D., D.D.S., D.V.M.	4	4	4	3	8	18
Business	20	12	38	30	11	15
Engineers	18	8	25	11	11	11
Social workers	16	8	2	3	26	19
Education	10	41	10	36	27	20
Government workers	10	10	3	7	5	2

	66 / 72	64 / 72	68 / 75	66 / 73	59 / 72	59 / 76
7. Occupational status[b]						
First job after graduation (average)	66	64	68	66	59	59
Current (1966) job (average)	72	72	75	73	72	76
8. Personal income (1966): Means						
In 1966 dollars	$11,550	11,650	13,580	12,960	10,960	11,700
In 1957–59 dollars[c]	10,217	10,304	12,011	11,459	9,642	10,349
Classes of 1931–1948	14,091	15,000	24,700	17,600	15,818	15,059
Classes of 1949–1954	12,979	12,821	16,146	14,273	13,280	14,148
Classes of 1955–1959	12,125	10,771	10,875	12,170	8,909	10,652
Classes of 1960–1964	9,000	8,552	9,651	8,700	7,977	7,313
9. Personal income (1966): Medians[c]	8,895	8,782	9,302	9,394	7,737	8,035
10. Income differences (white-black)						
Means	2,030[d]	1,310[e]			2,620[d]	1,260[e]
Means[c]	1,794	1,155			2,371	1,110
Medians[c]	407	612			1,565	1,358
11. Ratio of median black/white[c] (1966) incomes	.96	.93			.83	.85
12. Personal income (1966): Means[c]						
Employment sector						
Public	9,204	10,033	9,726	9,754	8,588	8,979
Private	12,710	11,328	13,183	14,302	13,120	13,281
Holders of						
Bachelor's degrees (only)	9,542	9,333	10,908	11,235	7,999	8,339
Postgraduate degrees	11,118	11,395	14,442	11,804	12,273	12,947

[a] All graduates, as such, had completed at least 16 years of school. Amount of graduate education is represented by the difference between total education and 16.

[b] Measured by Duncan's SES scale.

[c] Income figures are in 1957–59 dollars.

[d] Differences between ASU whites and this group of black graduates.

[e] Differences between MSU whites and this group of black graduates.

JOBS

3. *Business and the professions.* Since our respondents were college graduates, often with graduate degrees, we might well expect almost all to hold white-collar jobs, usually of a professional or managerial sort. However, previous writers (Turner, 1954; Broom and Glenn, 1965:143; Taeuber, 1967) have noted that blacks have found easier entrance into the professions than into the business world. This is a general finding, but it would be more strongly supported if replicated for college graduates.

To some extent our data upheld these findings. White graduates favor business occupations in greater percentages than black graduates; in addition, higher proportions of whites are in the "managers, officials, and proprietors" and "sales" categories than blacks. Yet a majority of *all* respondents—white *and* black—were principally engaged in the professions. Moreover, white MSU graduates chose professional over business jobs in a pattern more closely resembling that of their black classmates (and of ASU blacks) than that of ASU whites. Of all the black samples, Frazier graduates entered the professions by the greatest percentages and business by the smallest. Even at the college level, then, business (self-employed and salaried) still recruits disproportionately smaller numbers of blacks (relative to the professions); however, this finding is made somewhat ambiguous by MSU whites' job similarity to our black graduates.

The respective proportions of our black and white graduates in professional rather than managerial and business jobs are a little larger than those found in a 1963 national survey of 1958 B.A. degree holders (Sharp, 1970:66). Sharp found that 66 percent of 14,117 white, and 67 percent of 247 black, male graduates entered the professions, while only 22 percent of the white, and 12 percent of the black, graduates entered business or managerial positions. More of our graduates, particularly MSU whites and blacks and ASU whites, entered business positions than did graduates in Sharp's study. In addition, a larger proportion of our graduates, notably those from Frazier, entered the professions.

4 and 5. *Private and Public-Sector Employment.* The Census categories of jobs are useful because of their generality, but more specific classifications reveal more about our sample. Jobs can be described as in the *private sector* of the economy, or in the *public*. Those in the private sector can be further classified as self-employed (e.g., grocery store owner, barber) or salaried jobs (e.g., food store manager for a chain grocery, bank president); those in the public sector, as either nonprofit (e.g., educational researcher) or government

(social worker, administrator) jobs. The data show that white and black graduates from different schools are self-employed to about the same extent (10 to 13 percent), with ASU whites slightly more prone to self-employment. The patterns in the salaried jobs are not as similar. In this category (as with governmental jobs), the percentages vary widely between schools and racial groups. ASU graduates—white and black—are more inclined toward salaried jobs than are MSU graduates of the same race; however, ASU and MSU whites are more inclined toward these jobs than are ASU and MSU blacks. In addition, white ASU graduates were heavily recruited (about 55 percent) into salaried jobs.

The data also show that black graduates enter nonprofit jobs more often than white graduates, and MSU graduates enter them more often than ASU graduates. Furthermore, a majority of graduates in each black sample held government jobs; white MSU graduates closely resemble the blacks in this respect (with 49 percent in governmental jobs).

Overall, then, we should not be surprised to find that in general, black graduates hold public-sector jobs in larger proportions than white graduates, or that MSU graduates do so more than ASU graduates. The Frazier graduates fall somewhere between the ASU and MSU blacks: they enter the public sector to a greater extent than ASU blacks, and the private sector to a greater extent than MSU blacks.

6. *Specific Occupations.* A different breakdown of graduates' occupations reveals other differences among samples. All jobs held by graduates were assigned to a specific category.[10] Here we listed the percentages of each sample for those categories recruiting at least 11 percent (an arbitrary figure) of one or more samples. These categories are education, engineering, medical or dental practice, and business. First, among black graduates, MSU blacks show the highest percentage in *education.* Indeed, regardless of race a much higher percentage of MSU as opposed to ASU graduates is in education. The large proportions entering education may result from the educational orientation of MSU (although it is not known as a "teachers college") and hence may, in part, explain the unusually high percentage of MSU white graduates found in the professions (70 percent) and in the public sector (61 percent).

In general, ASU graduates were more likely than MSU graduates to become *engineers,* and whites more likely than blacks. The percentages suggest that certain combinations of school and racial groups are more (or less) likely to become engineers, quite apart from any general influence of race or school. For example, ASU whites seem a little more likely, and MSU blacks a little less likely, to become engineers than we would generally expect. The data showed surprisingly little difference between ASU and MSU whites and blacks (3 to 5 percent) entering *medicine*. However, Frazier graduates were strongly represented in medicine (particularly in the oldest cohort).

Social work is sometimes associated with blacks, and, indeed, we find larger percentages of blacks than whites in this field. Frazier has over twice the percentage of graduates in social work of ASU and MSU black graduates combined. Whites and ASU graduates generally were more inclined toward *business*, with the differences between whites and blacks clearly greater than those between ASU and MSU graduates. This finding helps to account for the large percentage of ASU whites (73 percent) holding salaried and self-employed jobs.

Finally, with regard to less popular occupations (not shown on Table 3.2), we observed that black ASU and MSU graduates entered *pharmacy* and *law* slightly more often than their white classmates. In addition, we found no overabundance of black *ministers* (in comparison with white), as some might have expected.

7.   The occupational analysis technique used most heavily in this book assigns status scores to jobs according to Duncan's socioeconomic index of occupations (see Appendix B; also Reiss et al., 1961; Blau and Duncan, 1967:12f).

We found modest differences between blacks and whites in average status of first job held after graduation. Frazier graduates' first jobs had slightly less status than those of white and black ASU and MSU graduates. Differences in the average status of their current (1966) jobs were similarly modest. A maximum of 3 current-job status units separated white and black graduates in any given comparison. Differences in average current-job status within the four cohorts of matched samples (whose average education was discussed above) rarely exceeded 5 status units and thus do not merit discussion.

The average status of these graduates' jobs is, of course, considerably greater than that of jobs held by men generally. Duncan (1969) reported averages (as of March, 1962) of 20 and 44 for black and white men of native origins, ages 25 to 64, of nonfarm background.

PERSONAL INCOME

Finally, we examine the differences between white and black mean incomes. Line 8 shows that the *average personal income* of graduates as of 1966, in terms of 1966 dollars, ranged between $11,000 and $13,500. White graduates averaged from $1200 to $2600 more than black graduates. If we take inflation between 1957–1959 and 1966 into account (by considering 1966 mean incomes in terms of 1957–59 dollars), the differences range from $1100 to $2371. The less recent a graduate's class, the greater his average income and that of his contemporaries (see figures for the average incomes of black and white graduates in the four cohorts). With one exception (ASU classes of 1955–1959), white graduates in each cohort consistently average more income than black graduates; the gap is widest for the smallest and oldest cohort of graduates (classes of 1931–1948) but narrows for the remaining three cohorts. The income gap for the most recent cohort is small between ASU and MSU classmates ($200–$600), but large ($1400–$1600) between the white groups and their matching Frazier graduates.

9. The *median incomes* of all groups of graduates are distinctly lower than their corresponding mean incomes. This finding indicates that incomes above the median are considerably more spread out than those below, thus pushing the means above the medians. Hence the mean, sensitive to this spread, tells a different story about graduates' success than the median, which is not sensitive to spreading. The mean figures reflect the degree to which many graduates were especially successful at achieving high incomes (that is, those moderately to considerably higher than the median figures).

10. The *median differences* are usually less than the mean income differences. Between ASU whites and their matching black groups, median differences range between $400 and $600, considerably less than the $1000 or more differences in mean incomes. Among MSU whites and their matching black groups, median income differences are more substantial (smaller in one comparison and larger in the other than the mean income difference). These results suggest that the above-median incomes of ASU whites are more widely spread than those of ASU blacks and Frazier–1 blacks; those of MSU whites are more widely spread than those of MSU blacks, but less widely spread than those of Frazier–1 blacks.

11. *The ratios of black to white median incomes* approach 1, especially for comparisons with ASU whites. The ratios here are much higher than the ratio for white and black college graduates nationally (0.69), just as our mean income differences are less than those for graduates nationally (see Table 2.1).

Line 12 shows the mean incomes and the corresponding gaps between black and white mean incomes of graduates with *public- versus private-sector employment* and of graduates holding bachelor's degrees only versus those holding postgraduate degrees. The data show that the graduates with private-sector employment and postgraduate education have the higher mean incomes. These differences are further analyzed at the close of Chapter 4.

SUMMARY

Whether we consider mean or median income levels, the data show that black graduates almost invariably receive less income than white graduates. Yet average current-job status for both groups is essentially equal, and blacks have completed more graduate education than whites. It appears, then, that black graduates actually needed more graduate education in order to obtain comparable jobs, which then paid less than those of their white classmates. One could object that the interpretation is not quite that simple. Our data (see lines 4, 5, and 6) show differences in the kinds of jobs that white and black graduates take. Risking sociological naiveté, we might say that black graduates simply select the kinds of jobs that pay less than those taken by whites. The fact remains, however, that admission to even these jobs followed the completion of more graduate education than was completed by whites entering better-paying jobs.

These findings, consisting largely of averages, are not a particularly sound basis for interpreting the relationships among these variables. We suggest cautiously that black graduates had "too much education," or more education than was needed, or were overqualified for the jobs and incomes they received. A corollary would be that the white graduates had "just enough" education to qualify for equally prestigious, better-paying jobs. We noted earlier that discrimination occurs where unequal rewards are received for equal qualifications. With respect to average incomes, then, what the data show are inferior rewards for superior qualifications! Finally, the equality of job status is somewhat surprising. This finding suggests that occupational status is a different kind of reward than income. In addition, it may indicate a modicum of equal success by black and white graduates, even if it took unequal amounts of graduate education (more for the blacks) to achieve this equality.

NOTES

1. We had noted that the proportions of graduates obtaining different kinds of degrees (e.g., B.A., theological, education) were not the same among whites and blacks in most years of graduation. Wherever possible, therefore, we constituted the pools of white graduates from which matching graduates were later drawn in such a way that the proportions of white and black graduates with different kinds of degrees were the same. This procedure—"frequency matching"—does not guarantee that each member of a matched pair has the same kind of degree, only that white members will not *consistently* have a different kind of degree than black members do.

For graduates whose family of origin was headed by their mothers rather than their fathers, or by other persons of either sex, the occupation of such heads of household was used.

2. These measures, respectively, are Astin's measures of "intellectualism" and "selectivity." The scores for these measures had a mean of 50 and a standard deviation of 10 (i.e., two-thirds of all scores fell between 40 and 60). The averages of these two measures for the three universities whose alumni we interviewed were 54.5 for the largely black university, and 55.5 and 56 for the two integrated universities. Spelman (43), Howard (52), and Morehouse (51.5) fell below these values; UNC–CH (58) and NYU (62) were above. On the same scale, Princeton was 70.5; Duke, 67; and Harvard, 77.

3. Usually the differences between samples were less than 5 percent, but our stated procedure was to combine samples if the differences were under 10 percent.

4. Five entries in Table 2.1 are based on numbers depleted by 10 or more instances of missing of unavailable information; for only 3 of these entries does the number of missing cases represent more than 10 percent of the original sample. Eighteen MSU blacks, 15 MSU whites, and 19 Frazier (MSU) blacks did not know their father's (or head of household's) educational level, and 12 MSU whites did not know their mother's education. Ten ASU and MSU blacks did not give information on father's birthplace.

5. Birthplaces were not rigorously classified. Graduates were asked, "Up to the age of 16 did you live mostly on a farm, in a village or small town, in a city, or in the suburbs of a city?" The graduates themselves determined whether their hometown was a "city," "suburb," or "small town"; this self-determination probably caused some classification (measurement) error. Very few answered "farm"; hence percentages for this response were omitted from Table 3.1.

6. Graduates were asked, "While you were growing up, did your (mother/mother substitute) *mostly* have a full-time job for which she was paid, have a part-time job, or did she mostly keep house?" If a graduate reported that his mother "mostly" had a full-time job, he was then asked, "What kind of work did she do mostly?" The response was coded using the Duncan socioeconomic index (our measure of occupational status; see Appendix B).

7. Graduates were asked, "Who were the adult males who lived in the household in which you lived *mostly* until you were 16 years old? That is, how were they related to you?" The categories that followed included "real father," "step-father," "adopted father," "foster father," "grandfather," "older brother," "other male relative," "male nonrelative," "no male in household," and "institution." Answers to a similar question about adult females completed our measure of "intactness."

8. Graduates were asked, "Which *one* of these sources contributed *most* to your (undergraduate) college costs?" Graduates chose their answers from a card listing possible responses.

9. As in the previous section, the row numbers in Table 3.2 correspond to the numbers preceding the paragraphs.

These assignments of years express our (perhaps) arbitrary judgment regarding the number of years of graduate education typically required to complete various degrees.

10. Some of these specific categories encompass a wide range of occupations. *Educational* occupations include secondary school teachers, principals, and other secondary school personnel; as well as college professors and other university personnel. *Health* occupations include medical and laboratory technicians and related personnel, and (a very few) undertakers. *Government* occupations include members of the armed forces, post office workers, and employees of government agencies not otherwise listed in category 6 (e.g., it excludes social workers). *Business* encompasses sales (wholesale and retail), insurance, real estate, public relations, marketing, advertising, publishing, journalism, banking and stock personnel, accountants, auditors, controllers, statisticians, finance analysts, managers, administrators, clerks, and other white-collar workers. *Other* includes farmers and craftsmen.

4

BLACKS' AND WHITES' INCOMES: DIFFERENCES AND DETERMINANTS_____

P art of this analysis examines the relationships between graduates' personal income and job status and three other income-producing resources—graduate education, years of experience since graduation (referred to simply as years of experience), and employment sector. We subsequently consider the effect of several additional variables on job status and income; this second analysis does not greatly alter the earlier findings. Finally, we take an abbreviated look at the effects of the principal, income-producing resources on the incomes of four subgroups of graduates.

MODEL

The assumptions underlying the first analysis are modeled in Figure 4.1. The relationships are presumed linear, and they have been estimated using regression analysis (ordinary least squares). Of the variables shown, several were defined in the previous chapter. Here we add "years of experience," a simple transformation of the year of college graduation. Because military service sometimes occurred subsequent to graduation, this measure is not identical to either the actual number of years in the labor force or to a man's age, but it correlates highly with both.[1] In this analysis, employment sector is

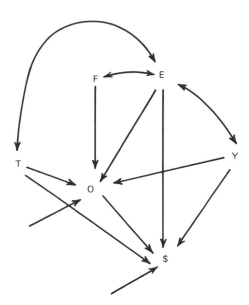

Figure 4.1 Model of the influence of income-producing resources on current-job status and personal income. F = first-job status; E = years of education leading to a degree; T = employment sector; Y = years of experience; O = current-job status; and $ = personal income.

a dummy variable created by assigning a score of +1 to a graduate employed in the private sector, and a 0 to a graduate employed in the public sector. (Hence if employment sector is positively related to income, graduates employed in the private sector earned more than those in the public sector.) The status of first job held after college graduation is scored using the same index of socioeconomic status used to score the graduates' current jobs. Other variables appearing in Tables 4.1 and 4.2 are defined and discussed later in this chapter.

As expressed in the model, the greater a graduate's first-job status, number of years taken to obtain his most advanced degree, and number of years of experience, the greater will be his current-job status. The status of private-sector jobs is also presumed to exceed that of public-sector jobs, and income (as of 1966, but stated in 1957–1959 dollars)[2] is presumed to vary directly with current-job status, years of experience, and graduate education. Finally, incomes from private-sector jobs should exceed those from public-sector jobs.

Note that first-job status is not presumed to affect a graduate's income directly; rather, status is presumed to exercise its greatest effect by influencing current-job status, which, in turn, affects current income. If first-job status had any important direct bearing on current income, independent of its effect through the status of the current job, then two graduates holding down current jobs of comparable status should show current-income differences that correspond to whatever first-job status differences exist. The data supported our presumption regarding this effect for all but one group of graduates (see below).

ANALYSIS OF TOTAL SAMPLE

The results of three regression analyses are shown in Table 4.1. Columns 1, 4, 7, 10, 13, and 16 of the income panel show unstandardized regression coefficients for a simple model in which income is solely a function of graduate education and job status. These are presented to emphasize the effect of adding years of experience and employment sector to the analysis (see columns 2, 5, 8, 11, 15, and 17).[3] The remaining columns are discussed later in this chapter.

INCOME VALUES OF RESOURCES

The coefficients in columns 2, 5, 8, 11, 14, and 17 indicate the income values of each resource. Income is in units of $1000. Thus among ASU whites, for example, a difference of one unit of job status corresponds to an average difference of $150 (0.15 × $1000). One year of graduate education (leading to a degree) adds an average of $620 per year. A graduate with 4 years' more experience than another should expect to average $2000 more a year (4 × 0.5 × $1000). Finally, a graduate working in the private sector can expect to average $3630 more a year than one in the public sector.

The meaning of the job status figures in these same columns is quite similar. They show the status values of each resource. One unit of status on the first job is worth 0.26 units of status on the current job. For example, two graduates whose first jobs differed by 4 units of status can expect a difference of about 1 unit in their current-job statuses. Three added years of graduate education corresponds to 8.58 added units of job status.

The range of each resource's absolute effects on income and job status, across groups of graduates, is quite broad. Two graduates who differ by 10 units of job status can expect their incomes to differ by as little as $400 or as much as $1500. If they differ by 2 years of graduate education (e.g., an M.A. degree versus a B.A. only), the average income difference can be as little as $460 or as much as $1940. Likewise, a difference of 4 years' experience can add between $760 and $2000 a year, on the average. Finally, a private-sector job could mean as much as $3630 or as little as $900 more than a public-sector job.

TABLE 4.1 THE INCOME, JOB-STATUS, AND GRADUATE-EDUCATION VALUES OF SEVERAL INDEPENDENT VARIABLES, AS MEASURED BY UNSTANDARDIZED PARTIAL REGRESSION COEFFICIENTS, FOR SIX GROUPS OF GRADUATES

Independent Variables	ASU Whites			ASU Blacks			Frazier-1 Blacks		
	(1)	(2)	(3)c	(4)	(5)	(6)c	(7)	(8)	(9)c
Income									
Current-job status[a]	.13[b]	.15	.11	.06*	.04	.04	.11	.07	.08
Graduate education	.81*	.62	.11	.41	.23	.28	1.32	.97	.86
Years of experience[d]		.50	.48		.19	.16		.21	.20
Employment sector		3.63	3.27		3.05	3.63		2.65	2.35
Father's education[e]			.18			−.12			−.01
Father's job status[e]			−.04			.02			.01
Cumulative grade average			4.65			.46			−.29
Father born abroad			2.44*			—			—
Intact family			—			—			−2.53
Rural-urban			—			1.74*			−2.04
Current-job status[a]									
First-job status	3.36			3.54			3.32		
Graduate education		.26	.23		.16	.13		.16	.20
Years of experience		2.86	2.56		2.97	2.96		2.37	1.93
Employment sector		−.06	−.07		.01	−.04		.14	.23*
Father's education		−1.01	−1.38		4.92	6.27		8.44	8.54
Father's job status			.47			−.22			−.34
Cumulative grade average			−.02			.11*			.00
Foreign-born			1.43			3.34			1.39
Intact family			—			29.9			—

	MSU Whites			MSU Blacks			Frazier-2 Blacks[f]		
Independent Variables	(10)	(11)	(12)	(13)	(14)	(15)	(16)	(17)	(18)
Graduate education									
Cumulative grade average			1.65			1.20			1.48
Father's education			.07*			.02			−.03
Father's job status			.01			.01			−.01
Father born abroad			—			—			1.74
Intact family			—			.78			—
Number of siblings			—			−.17			—
Income									
Current-job status	.09	.07*	.03	.12	.10	.10	.12	.13	.11
Graduate education	.40	.38	.25	.57	.39	.40	.98	.62	.38
Years of experience		.33	.36		.22	.22		.39	.39
Employment sector		3.62	3.54		.90	.83		2.17*	1.46
Father's education			.05			.08			.12
Father's job status			−.05			−.01			.07
Cumulative grade average			.95			.54			2.25
First-job status			.09						
Rural-urban			—			—			−2.12*
Current-job status									
First-job status	2.33	.15	.17	2.16	.31	.31	3.04	.09	.09
Graduate education		2.13	2.15		1.95	2.11		2.50	2.60
Years of experience		−.06	−.03		.32	.25		−.20	−.31
Employment sector		3.12	4.17		.74	1.96		6.77	6.31
Father's education			.77			−1.10			−.14

47

TABLE 4.1 (CONTINUED)

	MSU Whites			MSU Blacks			Frazier-2 Blacks[f]		
Independent Variables	(10)	(11)	(12)	(13)	(14)	(15)	(16)	(17)	(18)
Father's job status			−.18			.12			.00
Cumulative grade average			1.87			−.99			1.11
Father born abroad			—			10.36			10.55*
Foreign-born			—			—			8.47
Religion			—			—			
Graduate education									
Cumulative grade average			.14			.52			1.16*
Father's education			−.05			.01			.00
Father's job status			.00			.00			.02
Father born abroad			−.49*			—			—
Intact family						.60			—

[a] As of 1966; income adjusted in terms of 1957–1959 dollars.

[b] Underlined coefficients are significant at <.05; those marked by an asterisk are significant at .10 > p > .05. For a discussion of significance as used in the research, see Appendix C.

[c] Coefficients indicate the effect of the named variable when all other variables, including those listed on p. 61-2, are taken into account. The following variables are listed only when their coefficients were significant at <.10: first-job status, father born abroad, foreign-born, intact family, number of siblings, religion, rural-urban, southern-born.

[d] See text for discussion of this measure.

[e] Data on other head of household used when data on father were not available.

[f] The Ns for each sample are shown in Table 3.1.

TABLE 4.2 COMPONENTS OF MEAN PERSONAL INCOME DIFFERENCES, WHEN INCOME IS DETERMINED BY GRADUATE EDUCATION, CURRENT-JOB STATUS, EMPLOYMENT SECTOR, AND YEARS OF EXPERIENCE[a]

Components Reflecting	ASU Whites ASU Blacks	ASU Whites Frazier-1 Blacks	MSU Whites MSU Blacks	MSU Whites Frazier-2 Blacks
A. Differences in mean				
Graduate education	−97	−322	−114	−500
Employment sector	988	1284	157	102
Years of experience	−3	−45	−17	121
Current-job status	111	234	62	−411
Subtotal of A	999	1151	88	−689
B. Differences in income value of				
Graduate education	355	−321	−20	−254
Employment sector	421	711	1051	557
Years of experience	2708	2543	1080	−627
Current job-status	2693	1933	−841	−1354
Subtotal of B	6177	4866	1270	−1678
C. Other (including racial) differences	−5381	−3647	−203	3477
Mean income difference	1795	2370	1155	1110

[a] The zero points for this decomposition were as follows: job status, 50 units; years of experience, 2 (since 1964 was the last class studied); employment sector, 0 (public-sector work); graduate education, 16 years = 0.

Moving now to the second panel of Table 4.1, we see that a difference of 10 first-job status units corresponded to between 0.9 and 3.1 units of added current-job status. Two years' more education added an average of 3.9 to 5.94 additional units of status. For all practical purposes, increasing years of experience did not bring added job status. In general, public-sector jobs carried a little less status (between .74 and 8.44 units) than private-sector jobs.

One pattern that emerges from these numbers is that white graduates generally, but not always, receive more added income than blacks from the possession of additional resources. Working in the private rather than the public sector is always worth more for white graduates than for black. With one exception (Frazier–2 blacks versus MSU whites), added years of experience brings more additional income to white than to black graduates. Conversely, additional graduate education brings more income to *black* graduates in all but one comparison (ASU whites versus all blacks). Finally, job status has more income value for white ASU graduates than for either ASU or Frazier–1 blacks, but less for white MSU graduates than for MSU or Frazier–2 blacks.

The findings evident in the job-status coefficients are less interesting and display few patterns. If we compare the effects of first-job status, graduate education, and employment sector for MSU and Frazier–2 blacks and MSU whites, the whites' resources have a status value intermediate to that of the black graduates. In contrast, when black men are matched to white ASU graduates, first-job status has greater status value for whites than for either black group. Furthermore, graduate education has almost as much or more status value for ASU whites than for their matched blacks. Finally, the public-sector jobs of ASU blacks and Frazier–1 blacks have more status value than jobs in the private sector, while the opposite finding held for ASU whites.[4]

DECOMPOSING THE INCOME GAP

We now know that some groups of black and white graduates differ markedly with regard to the average income value of certain resources. Groups also differ with respect to average characteristics (for example, the proportion of men entering private- rather than public-sector jobs). The question now is: how does the combination of these differences affect average differences in mean incomes? Component analysis provides the answers. The results of this analysis are shown in Table 4.2.[5] The analysis examines three components and the subcomponents of each.

The A Component. Each of the *A subcomponents* shown in Table 4.2 represents the dollar contribution of differences in the average resources of black and white graduates to the mean income gap between whites and blacks. Differences in the average level of graduate education favor black graduates; these negatively signed differences offset the positively signed contributions (favoring white graduates) of differences in other factors, though usually by small amounts. Differences in average years of experience and in average current-job status usually account for modest amounts of the income gap.[6]

The principal finding here (for two of the four comparisons) is the effect of the difference in the proportions of white and black graduates employed in the private rather than the public sector. As was noted earlier, a much larger proportion of white than black ASU graduates is employed in the better-paying private sector; conversely, a much larger percentage of ASU and Frazier–1 black graduates is employed in the less remunerative public sector. The result of this situation is a difference of $1000 or more in mean incomes. In contrast, only minor differences separate MSU whites from MSU blacks (or from Frazier–2 blacks) working in the private sector, and these differences contribute little to the income gap. We should note, though, that Frazier–2 black graduates' greater average graduate education—in comparison with MSU whites—corresponds to $500, more than enough to offset other, positively signed contributions to the income gap.

The B Component. Between ASU whites and their black counterparts, differences in the extent to which additional experience and occupational status produce income cause very large differences between white and black average incomes. These two factors together dominate the subcomponents producing the income gap between ASU white and ASU and Frazier–1 black graduates. For these groups, employment sector, years of experience, and current-job status together accounted for more than $500 of the mean differences in incomes. Whites consistently benefited more from private-sector employment, but blacks benefited more as job status increased across individuals. MSU whites' incomes diverged from MSU blacks', but converged with that of Frazier–2 blacks, with increasing years of experience.

Across all components, the greater income value of graduate education usually accruing to black graduates affects the income gap by less than $400. Whites' incomes diverge from blacks' (the range is from $400 to $1000) by benefiting more than blacks' from private-sector employment (quite apart from the fact that whites are so employed more frequently, as we found when analyzing the *A subcomponents*). Also, whites' incomes usually diverge from blacks' (by over $2000) with increasing years of experience. Finally, the greater income value of white (ASU) or black (MSU and Frazier–2) graduates' job statuses corresponds to uniformly substantial contributions—in excess of $800—to the various income gaps.

The C Component. The *C component* represents the gap (which, if positively signed, favors whites) in incomes among men with B.S. degrees, 2 years of experience, 50 units of job status, and public-sector employment. Very few graduates are actually so characterized.[7]

The sum of the *C* and *B components*, as it turns out, is the gap in mean incomes between whites and blacks with the average level of graduate education, years of experience, and job status of all the white graduates in a given comparison, and with a value on employment sector equal to the proportion of all whites in the private sector. Across the four comparisons, in order, this sum comes to $796, $1219, $1067, and $1678 (figures not shown in Table 4.2). The individual sums and their average—over $1100—are substantial.

By comparing this sum with the mean income gap, we can depict the overall covergence or divergence of white and black incomes as graduate education and other resources increase across individuals. To do so for each comparison that follows, we calculated the income gap for hypothetical pairs of white and black graduates with "modest" and "considerable" resources. For example, a pair of graduates who are public-sector social workers with 4 years' experience and B.A. degrees (social workers' status score is 64), and a pair of public-sector school teachers (status score 72) with B.A. degrees and 8 years' experience exemplify graduates with modest resources. Likewise, a pair of private-sector lawyers (status score 93) with 3-year law degrees and 12 years' experience, and a pair of private-sector doctors (status score 92) with medical degrees and 13 years' experience, exemplify graduates with considerable resources.[8]

When ASU and Frazier–1 black graduates are matched to white ASU graduates (the three samples together are here referred to as the ASU group—with apologies to Frazier graduates), we find substantial income divergence as we move from graduates with modest resources to those with considerable resources (see Figure 4.2).[9] The decomposition tells us that (1) the white graduates' advantages from the greater income value of added experience and job status and (2) the larger proportions of whites employed in the private sector contribute most heavily to this divergence.

Furthermore, contrasting the sum of the *B* and *C components* and the mean income gap suggests that some black graduates whose average resources are less than those of average white graduates are doing almost as well (with regard to income) as whites with comparable resources, and maybe a little better: the income gap between (hypothetical) whites and blacks possessing the average amount of resources for black graduates is just under $500, but the incomes of (hypothetical) black graduates with modest resources exceed those of comparable whites by anywhere from $226 to $3000. By the same token, the gap between white and black graduates with considerable resources is enormous and favors whites. The expected gap between graduates with considerable resources ranges from $1610 (between ASU black and Frazier–1 M.D's) to over $5000 (between ASU white and black M.D.'s).

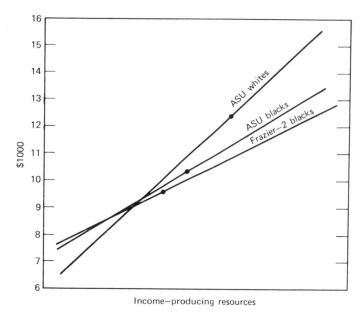

Figure 4.2   A Representation of the component analysis of the ASU-group income gaps.

The picture for the MSU group is more complex. Comparing MSU white graduates and Frazier–2 black graduates provides a sharp and interesting contrast to the diverging incomes found above (see Figure 4.3). A positive *C component* and a negative *B component* tell us that, overall, white and black incomes *converge* across graduates as their resources increase. In addition, Frazier–2 black graduates have a $689 advantage over MSU whites because, on the average, they have completed more graduate education and hold slightly higher-status jobs. However, complete convergence occurs for only a few Frazier–2 black graduates at best (the gap for hypothetical M.D.'s is about $200; for lawyers, about $1000). The gap increases for graduates with resources comparable to those of average Frazier–2 black graduates ($1362) and MSU white graduates ($1799), and increases still further for most graduates with modest resources (for social workers, the gap is $2513, for example). Here it is the income of black graduates of modest resources (Frazier–2) that shows the most dramatic divergence.

Overall, incomes for white and black graduates in the MSU group diverge as in the ASU group, though not as dramatically. Some blacks with modest resources do as well as or a little better than whites with the same resources (the hypothetical black social workers and teachers earn $350 and $500 more

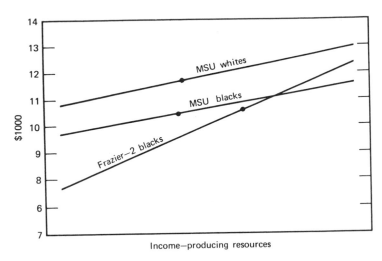

Figure 4.3   A representation of the component analysis of the MSU-group income gaps.

than their white counterparts). As individuals' resources increase, though, the gap favors whites (by $620 among men with resources similar to those of an average black MSU graduate, and by $1067 among men with resources comparable to those of average white MSU graduates). The gap increases to roughly $2000 for graduates with considerable resources. Like the ASU group comparison, this overall outcome is a compromise of opposing tendencies for incomes to converge, as some resources such as employment sector and years of experience increase, but to diverge as others, such as job status, increase.

On balance, the analysis suggests that relative to white graduates, there are either negative or, at best, qualified positive, objective incentives for blacks to increase their income-producing resources in earlier stages of their careers. ASU blacks have not been paid as much for additional job status or years of experience as comparable white classmates. Furthermore, if black graduates had resources equal to or below the average of white classmates, they were already doing as well as, if not better than, similarly endowed white classmates. Black MSU alumni fared similarly. Frazier–2 graduates narrowed the gap considerably but not completely, and only after many years of experience and the acquisition of high-status jobs.

We do not mean to suggest that black graduates have made conscious decisions about their jobs or level of education because they know or care about closing (or widening) the gap between their incomes and those of white classmates; we made no attempt to study such knowledge or concern.

However, even the complete absence of knowledge about any link between such factors and income does not alter the character or importance of the objective structure of incentives reviewed here. We are not dealing with the subjective experience of discrimination or with reports (confirmed or not) that some or all of our black sample members experienced instances of discrimination. *Unequal income values of resources, or more than modest income differences between graduates of different racial groups, possessing comparable resources, is prima facie evidence of discrimination*, whether perceived or not.

One observation on the above analysis should be made. Our discussion of income-gap components is obviously relative to the specific group of white graduates found in each comparison—hence the different patterns of positive and negative components found among Frazier–1 and –2 graduates. The subsamples are composed of somewhat different kinds of graduates; neither is representative of either all Frazier graduates or a random subsample of all such graduates. However, the differences between Frazier–1 and Frazier–2 graduates noted above are partly a function of *the particular group of white graduates to which they are compared*. As we noted in Chapter 3, these two white groups are quite different in their social characteristics; also, they probably work in different occupational and urban milieus.

RELATIVE EFFECTS OF RESOURCES

We now examine the relative effects on graduates' incomes of graduate education, job status, employment sector, and years of experience, and the relative effects of graduate education and years of experience on their job status. Where the previous analysis (using unstandardized regression coefficients) revealed the absolute income value (in dollars) of various resources and the dollar effects of three components on income, this analysis (using standardized coefficients) shows the relative effects of various resources in determining graduates' incomes.[10] The relevant data are shown in Tables 4.3 and 4.4.

We first find that graduate education determines job status to a consistently greater degree than it does income.[11] This is consistent with Duncan's earlier findings regarding the relative effects of schooling on job status and incomes for white men generally (Duncan, 1969). Second, the relative effect of job status on income was noticeably greater than that of graduate education for ASU white and MSU black graduates, and slightly greater for ASU black, MSU white, and Frazier–2 graduates. For Frazier–1 blacks, though, graduate education had relativey more direct influence than job status on income. On

TABLE 4.3 RELATIVE EFFECTS ON INCOME AND JOB STATUS OF SEVERAL INDEPENDENT VARIABLES, AS MEASURED BY STANDARDIZED PARTIAL REGRESSION COEFFICIENTS, FOR SIX GROUPS OF GRADUATES

Independent Variables	ASU Whites			ASU Blacks			Frazier-1 Blacks		
	(1)	(2)	(3)c	(4)	(5)	(6)c	(7)	(8)	(9)c
Income[a]									
Current-job status[a]	.21[b]	.24	.18	.16*	.10	.10	.21	.14	.16
Graduate education	.15*	.12	.02	.14	.08	.09	.40	.30	.26
Years of experience[d]		.43	.41		.25	.22		.24	.23
Employment sector		.19	.17		.28	.33		.18	.16
Father's education[e]			.07			–.08			–.00
Father's job status[e]			–.09			.08			.02
Cumulative grade average			.24			.04			–.02
Father born abroad			.15*						—
Intact family			—			—			–.18
Rural-urban			—			.15*			–.15
Residual path coefficient	.95	.82	.76	.96	.89	.85	.84	.80	.74
Current-job status[a]									
First-job status	.39	.31	.28	.46	.23	.18	.50	.30	.35
Graduate education		.33	.30		.38	.38		.36	.29
Years of experience		–.03	–.04		.00	–.02		.08	.13*
Employment sector		–.03	–.05		.18	.22		.29	.29
Father's education[e]			.11			–.06			–.11
Father's job status[e]			–.02			.15*			.00
Cumulative grade average			.04			.11			.04
Foreign-born						.19			—

Independent Variables	MSU Whites			MSU Blacks			Frazier-2 Blacks		
	(10)	(11)	(12)	(13)	(14)	(15)	(16)	(17)	(18)
Intact family									−.14*
Religion						.17			—
Residual path coefficient	.92	.87	.77	.89	.84	.78	.87	.76	.72
Income									
Current-job status	.17[a]	.13*	.06	.36	.31	.28	.20	.22	.19
Graduate education	.10	.09	.06	.21	.14	.15	.31	.20	.12
Years of experience		.33	.37		.30	.30		.32	.32
Employment sector		.28	.28		.08	.08		.14*	.09
Father's education			.03			.09			.07
Father's job status			−.13			−.02			.19
Cumulative grade average			.05			.04			.10
First-job status			.23			—			—
Rural-urban			—			—			−.12*
Residual path coefficient	.97	.85	.82	.89	.84	.81	.89	.83	.76
Current-job status									
First-job status	.30	.20	.23	.27	.41	.42	.57	.16	.15
Graduate education		.27	.28		.24	.26		.47	.49
Years of experience		−.03	−.02		.15	.12		−.10	−.15
Employment sector		.13	.17		.02	.06		.25	.23
Father's education			.24			−.35			−.05
Father's job status			−.27			.16			−.01

TABLE 4.3 (CONTINUED)

Independent Variables	MSU Whites			MSU Blacks			Frazier-2 Blacks		
	(10)	(11)	(12)	(13)	(14)	(15)	(16)	(17)	(18)
Cumulative grade average			.05			−.02			.03
Father born abroad			—			.14^e			—
Foreign-born			—			—			.13*
Religion			—			—			.15
Residual path coefficient	.95	.92	.87	.96	.86	.80	.82	.75	.73

[a] As of 1966; income adjusted in terms of 1957–59 dollars.

[b] Underlined coefficients are significant at <.05; those marked by an asterisk are significant at .10 > p > .05. For a discussion of significance as used in the research, see Appendix C.

[c] Coefficients indicate the effect of the named variable when all other variables, including those listed on p. 61-2, are taken into account. The following variables are listed only when their coefficients were significant at <.10: first-job status, father born abroad, foreign-born, intact family, number of siblings, religion, rural-urban, southern-born.

[d] See text for discussion of this measure.

[e] Data on other head of household used when data on father were not available.

TABLE 4.4   DIRECT AND SELECTED INDIRECT EFFECTS OF SEVERAL VARIABLES ON INCOME AND CURRENT-JOB STATUS, FOR SIX GROUPS OF GRADUATES

Effects	ASU Whites	ASU Blacks	MSU Whites	MSU Blacks	Frazier–1 Blacks	Frazier–2 Blacks
Current-job status[a]						
Graduate education (direct effect)	.33[b]	.38	.27	.24	.36	.47
First-job status (direct effect)	.31	.23	.20	.41	.30	.16
Income[a]						
Graduate education (direct effect)	.12	.08	.09	.14	.30	.20
Indirect through: current-job status	.08	.04	.04	.07	.05	.10
employment sector	−.03	.04	.03	.01	.04	.04
years of experience	.03	.05	.06	.07	.10	.07
Total	.20	.21	.22	.29	.49	.41
First-job status						
Indirect through current-job status	.07	.02	.03	.13	.04	.04
Current-job status (direct effect)	.24	.10	.13	.31	.14	.22
Indirect through employment sector	.00	.05	.04	.00	.05	.04
Years of experience (direct effect)	.43	.25	.33	.30	.24	.32
Employment sector (direct effect)	.19	.28	.28	.08	.18	.14
Sum of the selected indirect effects of education and first-job status on income, through current-job status	.15	.06	.07	.20	.09	.14

[a] Job status and income as of 1966; income adjusted in terms of 1957–59 dollars.
[b] The underlined standardized regression coefficients are significant at <.10.

59

the basis of earlier findings (Duncan, 1969), we had expected job status to be the stronger determinant for whites, and graduate education the stronger for blacks. Thus our findings for Frazier–1 blacks and ASU whites, but not for the other groups of graduates, are roughly consistent with earlier findings. However, the link between graduate education and income appears relatively more crucial for Frazier graduates than for the other groups: only for Frazier graduates are the (1) direct effect of education on job status and (2) direct and indirect effects of education on income greater than all other effects studied.

With two exceptions, the direct effect of graduate education on income is twice that of its indirect effect through job status: for ASU whites the ratio is 1.5; for Frazier–1, 6. For white graduates this finding contrasts markedly with the finding of an earlier study that the indirect effect is greater than the direct for white men generally, while the direct effect exceeded the indirect for black men generally. In addition, while our black graduates' incomes resemble those of black men generally in showing greater direct than indirect dependence on education, they still do not depend as heavily on the direct effects of education as do those of black men nationally (Frazier–1 graduates excepted).

Table 4.4 also shows that a graduate's current-job status is relatively more important as a determinant of income for MSU blacks than for any other group. First, status has a greater direct effect relative to that of other resources on income. Second, the size of the indirect effects of graduate education and of first-job status on current income is relatively greater than for other samples. In short, for this group job status is an especially important variable both in its own right and as a resource through which other resources can influence income. Table 4.4 also shows that for black ASU and white MSU graduates, employment sector has a relatively strong impact on incomes.[12]

Of all the factors affecting income, years of experience was generally the most influential. For white graduates its impact was greater than that of any other variable; for other groups of graduates, it was at least the second or third most important influence on income. Finally, the general effect of first-job status on either current-job status or income was less than the effect of graduate education on either.[13]

In general, the central resource in the network of variables affecting income—job status—lacks the relative impact we might have expected. MSU black graduates excepted, job status is a weak link in the chain, lessening the potential indirect effect of graduate education or first-job status. In a sense, then, this finding shows dissipation of the potential benefits to a graduate's income portended by strong links between resources such as graduate education and current-job status *when they exist*. Sometimes this waste is partly overcome when, as for Frazier graduates, graduate education has a relatively great direct influence on current-job status and income. This influence partly compensates for the weak connection between job status and income.

The optimal situation would find an anterior resource, such as graduate education, strongly affecting other resources intermediate to income, such as current-job status, if and only if the intermediate resources strongly influence income.[14] Resources that both significantly affect income directly *and* are strongly influenced by other resources can pass this influence on to income in a less diminished form than might otherwise be the case. Such resources are obviously preferable to those that strongly affect income without this combination of direct and indirect effects. Unfortunately, such combinations seem largely absent in the data just analyzed.

ADDITIONAL RESOURCES/SOCIAL CHARACTERISTICS

We now examine additional resources or social characteristics that might possibly affect either income or current-job status. Most of these variables are fully described in Chapter 3:

1. *Father's job status*: father's (or head of household's) principal occupation as scored by the Duncan index of socioeconomic status.

2. *Father's education*: father's (or head of household's) number of completed years of schooling.

3. *Cumulative grade-point average*: measured using the cumulative average of grades received by the graduate during his four years of college work (coded A = 1, B = 2 . . . F = 5).

4. *Father born abroad*: graduates with foreign-born fathers were scored 1; the remainder, 0.

5. *Foreign-born*: U.S.-born were coded 1; foreign-born, 0[15].

6. *Intact family*: graduates who lived with both natural parents until the age of 16 were coded 1; the others, 0.

7. *Number of siblings*: coded 0 for no siblings; 1 for one, and so forth.

8. *Religion*: here defined with respect to the hypothesis discussed by sociologists of religion (e.g., Lenski, 1961; Greeley and Rossi, 1966) that Catholics would be less successful than Protestants (non-Catholics were coded 1; Catholics, 0).

9. *Rural-urban*: (urban-born were coded 1; rural, 0)[16].

10.   *Southern-born*: those born in mid- or deep-south states were coded 0; those from border and other states and from abroad, 1^{17}.

11.   *First-job status*: scored using Duncan's index.

The analysis using these 11 variables (see Table 4.1) was directed toward answering two questions. First, what would be the effect on our earlier analysis of controlling for these additional variables, and which (if any) of these added factors would have a marked effect on current-job status or income? With regard to the first question, the analysis showed surprisingly little effect. For each column set in Table 4.1, compare the third column of coefficients for each sample with the second.

In only a few instances did the additional variables have any noticeable effects. When these occurred, they implied that our original estimate of resource P's effect on income or current-job status has confounded the effects of P (one of the original variables) with that of another variable, Q (introduced and controlled in this analysis). It follows, then, that the effects of P controlled for Q and of Q are both represented by the earlier estimate of P's effect. Hence, controlling for grades is primarily responsible for the lower estimate of the effect of graduate education on income among ASU white and Frazier–2 black graduates; that is, in the earlier analysis, especially for ASU whites, graduate education included the effects of both itself *and* of grades. Second, controlling for grades is also primarily responsible for the slightly reduced estimates of the effect of graduate education on job status among ASU white and Frazier–1 blacks (yet grade average per se had little influence on job status). Third, controlling for first-job status largely accounts for reducing the effect of graduate education on the income of MSU whites. Finally, controlling for first-job status modestly reduces the apparent influence of current-job status on white graduates' income.

Overall, then, the 11 additional variables have little general, independent effect on status or income, although there are a few noticeable differences between samples with respect to which specific variables have a noticeable influence. Finally, there is less than complete consistency regarding the direction of the effects of the same variable on either income or current-job status. To elaborate these last two findings, whether a graduate was born in or outside of an urban area affects ASU black and Frazier graduates, but in different ways. Urban ASU black graduates had higher incomes, but so did Frazier graduates with rural home towns! Or, coming from an intact family apparently helped MSU black graduates complete additional graduate education, but among Frazier–1 graduates, those from nonintact families had better jobs and higher incomes.

Likewise, ASU whites who are sons of immigrants earn an average of $2440 more than sons of U.S.-born Americans. MSU black graduates whose fathers were born abroad had better jobs—by about 10 status points. Second-generation Frazier–1 blacks went further in graduate school than sons of U.S.-born Americans, but M.S.U white sons of U.S.-born fathers completed more schooling than second-generation sons. For two groups, religion and foreign birth showed the same effect on graduates' job status: among ASU black and Frazier–2 black graduates, both U.S-born and non-Catholic graduates held better jobs.

Contrary to findings from previous research, the education and current-job status of graduates' fathers rarely had important effects on graduates' status and income. Only once is either a noticeable determinant of income—for Frazier–2 black graduates—and neither has any particular effect on completing graduate education. This result suggests that for these men, completing college has been a great equalizer. Those from humbler origins are probably underrepresented among graduates of these colleges, but if and when the less privileged (be they white or black) graduate, factors other than family background have determined whatever differences in income exist among classmates. Whether this situation results from college education per se or rather from the ability and determination required to have graduated from college, we cannot say.

Among MSU white and black graduates, fathers' education and job status noticeably affected their sons' current-job status, but this finding must be qualified. Most studies have found a positive relationship between father's position and son's achievement (although Blum, 1972, provides an exception)—the better the father's job (or the more education he had), the better (or more) the son's. Our data show just the reverse: The less education the fathers of MSU black graduates completed, and the lower the job status of white MSU graduates' fathers, the *better* their son's jobs. Finally, grade-point average strongly affects the incomes of white ASU graduates; those with the higher averages complete more graduate education, as do Frazier–2 black graduates.

We also analyzed the effects of grades, father's education, and job status on the attainment of graduate degrees. As is shown in Table 4.1, father's education and job status have a negligible effect on whether these men, once graduated, pursue and attain a postgraduate degree. However, for white and

Frazier graduates, such degrees were more likely to be attained by men with higher grade averages.

For these inconsistent and often puzzling results, varying as they do by groups of graduates, we can offer only partial explanations. Self-selection processes within the different samples could be responsible (see Appendix A). For example, recall that the Frazier–1 blacks from nonintact families made more money and held better jobs than those from intact families. Presumably the graduates from nonintact families demonstrated other qualities, such as determination, in compensating for the disadvantages of their background, which helped them to do better than their classmates from intact families.

However, the self-selection explanation becomes less persuasive when applied to several findings simultaneously. For self-selection to explain why nonurban Frazier blacks earn higher incomes than those from urban areas, or why grades noticeably affect the incomes of only two groups of graduates, we would have to specify a different process for each finding. It is difficult to believe that self-selection processes could be sufficiently varied and dissimilar to explain such diverse findings.

The other explanation addresses some of the variability in significant variables from group to group. Characteristics such as foreign birthplace, religion, or rural-urban (all scored 1, 0) are more likely to be significant influences on income, the more they vary within a group of graduates. The fact that half of our white graduates were second-generation sons of foreign-born fathers was, in part, the reason for the observed effect of father's birthplace on white graduate's incomes. This factor had little effect on black graduates' incomes because most of their fathers were U.S.-born. This kind of explanation accounts reasonably for some of the diverse results.[18]

The important result of analyzing and controlling for the effects of 11 additional variables, of course, is that our earlier findings regarding income, graduate education, years of experience, and employment sector are well sustained.

SUBGROUP ANALYSIS

One final question may be asked. Is the earlier analysis also sustained when we consider the incomes of important subgroups of graduates (those employed in the public versus the private sector; those holdings only a B.A. versus those holding a postgraduate degree)? Are incomes in these groups differently influenced by the four principal resources considered earlier? Are the corresponding income gaps similarly decomposed? To answer this question we regressed income on years of graduate education, current-job status, and years of experience, separately, for graduates employed in each sector. We also regressed income on current-job status, years of experience, and employment sector for graduates with B.A. degrees only; for postgraduate degree holders we added years of postgraduate education to the list of resources affecting incomes. The results of this analysis are shown in Table 4.5.

Table 4.5 shows, first, that graduate education has consistently *more income value* in the private sector than in the public for every group of graduates. Had we (earlier) decomposed the mean income differences of public- and private-sector employees from the same group of graduates, this difference would have made an enormous contribution to the income gap. Second, job-status differences have consistently greater income value for men with postgraduate, as opposed to B.A. only, degrees. Also, employment sector usually makes more difference to the incomes of men with postgraduate degrees than of those with B.A. degrees only. Years of experience (in four of the six groups) has a similar effect. Finally, our ability to explain graduates' incomes from the resources possessed is dramatically greater for the group with postgraduate degrees than for the group with B.A. degrees only.

With regard to the *decomposition* of income gaps (Table 4.6), the question is whether our original decompositions still hold when done on important subgroups. First, the data show that the ASU group as a whole remains largely unaffected by subgroup analysis. Average incomes diverge as resources increase; and as before, increasing experience and current-job status are prominently responsible for the degree of divergence observed. More specifically, the contributions of differences in the average resources of whites and blacks to the mean income gap observed for private-sector employees and holders of B.A. and postgraduate degrees is worth noting. In the latter two groups (as in the original analysis), the greater proportion of whites in the private sector produces the dominant effect. However, because this analysis grouped graduates not by year of graduation but rather by education and employment sector, differences in average years of experience can make a greater contribution than in the earlier analysis. Hence, the apparently greater experience of blacks with both postgraduate degrees and public-sector employment usually narrows the respective income gaps. In the private sector, blacks' advantage (especially Frazier blacks') from completing more graduate education sometimes makes an enormous contribution to reducing the income gaps. Such differences were not as pronounced in the earlier component analysis, which did not separate graduates working in the two sectors.

TABLE 4.5 INCOME VALUE OF THE FOUR PRINCIPAL RESOURCES FOR FOUR SUBGROUPS OF GRADUATES

Resources	ASU Whites	ASU Blacks	MSU Whites	MSU Blacks	Frazier-1 Blacks	Frazier-2 Blacks
Private-sector employees						
Current-job status	.16ᵃ	.10	.15*	.03	.07	.08
Graduate education	.93	.28	.69	.86	1.70	1.07
Years of experience	.50	.12	.54	.21	.20	.70
Coefficient of determination	.33	.11	.26	.21	.35	.40
Public-sector employees						
Current-job status	.06	.02	.00	.15	.06	.08
Graduate education	−.01	−.15	−.06	.14	.40	.20
Years of experience	.51	.24	.23	.23	.17*	.13*
Coefficient of determination	.24	.25	.15	.40	.30	.09
B.A. only						
Current-job status	.10*	.02	.08	.02	.03	.05
Employment sector	3.40*	2.70	2.18	.40	1.16	−.84
Years of experience	.36	.08	.41	.12	.24	.19
Coefficient of determination	.20	.11	.19	.06	.22	.14
Postgraduate degree holders						
Current-job status	.41	.07	.04	.17	.09	.10
Graduate education	−.83	.07	.76	.10	1.19	1.12
Employment sector	2.45	3.30*	5.56	1.88	4.68	4.95
Years of experience	.98	.36	.24	.25	.16	.58
Coefficient of determination	.56	.31	.64	.43	.34	.33

ᵃ Underlined coefficients are significant at $p < .05$; those marked with an asterisk are significant at $.10 > p > .05$.

TABLE 4.6 COMPONENTS OF MEAN PERSONAL INCOME DIFFERENCES FOR FOUR SUBGROUPS OF GRADUATES[a]

Components Reflecting	ASU Whites and		MSU Whites and		ASU Whites and		MSU Whites and	
	ASU Blacks	Frazier-1 Blacks	MSU Blacks	Frazier-2 Blacks	ASU Blacks	Frazier-1 Blacks	MSU Blacks	Frazier-2 Blacks
	Private-sector Employees				Public-sector Employees			
A. Difference in mean								
Graduate education	−243	−2082	−553	−2040	−20	125	−20	−54
Years of experience	−15	−42	269	1358	−80	−140	−222	−116
Current-job status	−222	−446	20	−703	113	446	−24	−54
Subtotal of A	−480	−2570	−264	−1385	13	431	−266	−224
B. Difference in income value of								
Graduate education	499	−605	−151	−345	191	−527	−227	−290
Years of experience	3440	2702	3770	−1701	2,194	2,791	−31	849
Current-job status	1459	2197	3078	1824	1,140	3	−3161	−1718
Subtotal of B	5398	4294	6697	−222	3,525	2,267	−3419	−1159
C. Other differences	−4445	−1660	−3460	2628	−3,016	−1,560	3406	2158
Mean income difference	473	64	2973	1021	522	1,138	−279	775

TABLE 4.6—(CONTINUED)

Components Reflecting	ASU Whites and		MSU Whites and		ASU Whites and		MSU Whites and	
	ASU Blacks	Frazier-1 Blacks	MSU Blacks	Frazier-2 Blacks	ASU Blacks	Frazier-1 Blacks	MSU Blacks	Frazier-2 Blacks
	Private-sector Employees				Public-sector Employees			
	B.A. Only				Postgraduate Degree Holders			
A. Difference in mean								
Graduate education	1015	656	92	-142	-9	-328	-14	-1742
Employment sector	55	352	88	265	664	1,465	141	-659
Years of experience	102	114	20	-44	-236	-406	-176	-545
Current-job status					260	496	170	-614
Subtotal of A	1172	1122	200	79	679	1,227	121	-3560
B. Difference in income value of								
Graduate education	555	1771	825	1396	-854	-1,916	446	-252
Employment sector	2416	1002	2681	2079	-517	-1,351	983	162
Years of experience	1720	1486	1200	588	6,044	8,031	-176	-3613
Current-job status					11,078	10,320	-3413	-1828
Subtotal of B	4691	4259	4706	4063	15,751	15,084	-2052	-5531
C. Other differences	-4497	-2472	-3004	-1246	-13,107	-14,142	2340	7948
Mean income difference	1366	2909	1902	2896	3,323	2,169	409	-1143

[a] For zero points, see Table 4.2. However, when we decomposed the mean income gaps for those holding postgraduate degrees, the zero point on education was amended to 18 years = zero.

The general picture is not as clearly followed by the MSU group. The incomes values of resources vary more across these three samples; hence, the component analyses of the income gaps do not always tell the same story. For example, we found earlier that, overall, incomes of MSU white and Frazier–2 graduates converged as resources increased (the income values of all resources except employment sector were greater for Frazier–2 blacks). This same convergence is evident for groups of graduates employed in the public sector and holding postgraduate degrees; as before, the greater value to Frazier–2 black graduates of job status and years of experience (for postgraduates) lies behind this convergence. (Indeed, the combination of converging incomes and greater average resources of Frazier–2 blacks results in the Frazier–2 blacks' averaging over $1000 more income than their white counterparts.)

However, for two groups—private sector and B.A. degrees only—different pictures emerge. For the latter, whites' incomes are greater and diverge from blacks', as do ASU graduates' in general, and the income values of all resources are consistently greater for white graduates in *all* comparisons. For the private-sector group, incomes neither converge nor diverge; whites receive about $2400 more than blacks regardless of resources. Finally, consistent with our original findings, Frazier–2 graduates in the private-sector and postgraduate groups had a marked advantage because they had completed (on the average) more graduate education. However, this advantage is virtually nonexistent for the public-sector group and, by definition, is absent from the B.A.-only group.

Our original analysis showed that MSU whites' and blacks' incomes diverged moderately as resources increased. The present analysis supports this finding for the private-sector and B.A. groups, but the incomes of the postgraduate group converge very slightly. For the public-sector group, black incomes converge with and overtake white incomes (indeed, MSU black graduates have a slight mean-income edge over their white classmates).

In sum, the size of the income gaps, the contributions to these gaps of differences in mean resources, and the income values of resources vary somewhat within the four subgroups. More broadly, the principle question was whether the general picture presented earlier was essentially the same as that for four important subgroups. The analysis shows that the picture for ASU and Frazier–1 graduates remains unchanged. The picture for MSU and Frazier–2 graduates is more of an average or composite picture—a blend of pictures that differ among the four subgroups. However, if we compare the subgroup analysis with the original analysis, the latter's essential outlines resemble the former in three out of four comparisons for each of the four subgroups.

These variations in decomposition suggest that researchers should (1) look for similar variation in other studies using comparable data, and (2) theorize about why and where such variations make sense. Some possible explanations—together with discussion of the difficulties inherent in explaining these variations—are given in Chapter 7.

NOTES

1.   Posner (1970) found correlations of .80 and .95 between year of graduation, year of birth, and years in the labor force (the latter ascertained from the complete history of jobs held by the graduate). These correlations were calculated for all groups of graduates combined.

2.   As with current-job status, actual income is as of 1966; however, unless otherwise noted, income figures are always adjusted in terms of 1957–1959 dollars.

3.   Both sets of columns show the effects of each resource on income, holding constant the effects of the other resources included in that regression.

4.   Since the analysis in Chapter 3 showed very little difference in average job status between black and white graduates, this chapter examines only briefly the effect of each of these resources on job status.

5.   The assumptions underlying this particular decomposition are discussed in Appendix D.

6.   This finding was expected because (1) matching graduates within years of graduation eliminated virtually all such differences, and (2) differences between whites' and blacks' average job statuses were quite small (see Chapter 3).

7.   The larger the number of independent variables in the regression, the less the likelihood that there are units of analysis (here graduates) with values consistently at the lower extremes of their ranges. For the purposes of component analysis, the values of independent variables range upward from a lower extreme called the "zero point" (Table 4.2 defines the zero points).

8.   We chose these hypothetical pairings so that graduates with "modest" resources possessed fewer resources than the average for black or white graduates; graduates with "considerable" resources, more than the average.

9.   Figures 4.2 and 4.3 represent the results of component analysis and do not depict the regression of income on four variables (technically impossible on a two-dimensional page). However, for cases in which income is regressed on only one variable, a representation of the results of the component analysis and of the appropriate regression lines coincide.

10.   There is a simple way to contrast the information conveyed by unstandardized and standardized coefficients as used in this book. Unstandardized coefficients estimate the absolute effects of differences in the resources that graduates possess in terms of corresponding typical differences in income. They also estimate the income value that might be derived from an individual's or group's increasing its resources by one unit of a given resource, that is, the amount of that individual's or group's income that depends on one unit of that resource. Standardized coefficients, in contrast, tell us the degree to which individual's incomes can be estimated from each resource *relative to other resources*. In different samples or groups, the absolute effect of any given resource can have a different relative effect, depending on both the variances of each resource and of personal income in different samples or groups, and on the absolute effect of each resource on income in each group.

11.   Schoenberg (1972:4) recently argued that path coefficients should not be compared across equations even when they pertain to the same sample. We have not yet been persuaded of this (despite some friendly correspondence with Schoenberg), but we have tried to minimize the extent to which this discussion may be vulnerable to his argument if it is correct.

12.   Not incidentally, these were the two groups of men most evenly divided between the two sectors—about 40 percent in the private and 60 percent in the public sectors. Equal proportions from the public and private sectors permit the variance of either proportion to be at or near its maximum value. The larger the variance in an independent variable, the more variation in a dependent variable it may be able to explain.

13.   For MSU black graduates, the effect of first-job status on current-job status was noticeably greater than that of graduate education (.41 > .24), however, and its indirect effect on income (through current-job status) equaled the direct effect of graduate education on income.

14.   "Optimal" from the viewpoint of the successful investment of resources, but not from the perspective that the possession of such resources becomes an exclusive means to income.

15.   The coding was arbitrarily different from that used for fathers in order to make the relationships between these variables and income or current-job status positive (most of the time).

16.   Suburban, small-town, and farm home towns (see Chapter 3) were considered "rural."

17.   Two other variables were originally included and then discarded. The *skin color* (light, medium, dark, very dark) of graduates had no effect on income or job status and, presumably, no effect on the interviews (NORC, which did these interviews, matched the race of interviewer and interviewee).

The educational level of graduates' mothers was also dropped because of its often strong correlation with father's education. Whatever one's theory about the likely impact of each parent's respective educational level, correlations between these levels on the order of .5 (observed for these data) suggest that their effects on dependent variables are quite redundant. For this and a related reason (that artificial results are quite possible in this situation), we omitted the educational level of one parent (see Coleman et al., 1972:303).

A third variable—birth order of graduate—was studied by Chapman (1970). She found that, in general, this variable had no relation to graduates' achievements; it was thus not included in the present analysis.

18.   Such factors as foreign birth and religion are, however, noticeable determinants of job status for two black samples (ASU and Frazier–2), in which 5 percent or fewer were either Catholic or foreign-born. The findings suggest considerable differences between the lower current-job status of a few Catholic or foreign-born graduates and others, taking other factors into account. But the small proportion of Catholic or foreign-born graduates in these groups makes these relationships less impressive than they might have been had a larger minority been Catholic or foreign-born.

5

GRADUATES' FAMILIES, WIVES' CHARACTERISTICS, AND FAMILY INCOME_____

In previous chapters we treated personal income as a measure of the return a graduate has received from his various income-producing resources. One such resource that we have not yet discussed is marital status. According to a recent analysis of 1960 Census data (Farley and Hermalin, 1971), "men of both races who were married-spouse-present had larger incomes than men who were single, married-spouse-absent, widowed or divorced." The same finding may well hold for our graduates, 75 percent or more of whom were married and living with their wives. In addition, many of these graduates had working wives. For them, family income is a better measure of the ability to consume goods and services than is husband's income alone. This chapter analyzes the family incomes of our married graduates.

Given our initial concern with the comparative influence of education, experience, and other resources on personal incomes, the first question that arises concerns the *relative* impact of husbands' and wives' occupational endeavors on their families' incomes. For black and white families, the relative income value of both husbands' and wives' resources, and the likelihood of wives' working, may well differ. These factors may, in turn, affect the size of the family-income gap separating white and black graduates.

We could expect this gap to be smaller than the personal-income gap previously discussed to the extent that (1) black graduates' wives held jobs more frequently than white graduates' wives, and (2) the former's resources brought at least the same income as the latter's. Certainly general evidence supports this expectation. A greater proportion of black than white women are in the labor force;[1] likewise, black wives work for pay more often than white wives (Carter and Glick, 1970). In addition, the income earned in 1969 by black women with one or more years of college is greater than that earned by white women with an equivalent education (about 120 percent of white income), though as of 1959 black women with this same amount of education earned slightly less (90 percent of white income; see Farley and Hermalin, 1972). As of 1966, the incomes of women in both categories were probably equal.

Other recent census data also support this expectation. While the differences (all favoring whites) in median family incomes for all blacks and whites within four age groups (25–34 . . . 55–64) increased between 1959 and 1969, the gap between *husband-wife families* and *single-parent households* declined in the same period. (The one exception was families headed by husbands aged 45–54.) The decline was especially dramatic (from $1739 to $980) for young families whose husbands were 25 to 34 years old (U.S. Burean of the Census, 1971a: Table 2). Furthermore, if we consider only husband-wife families of all ages, the black-white gap decreased in the 1959–1969 interval for families in which both spouses worked, but increased when only the husband worked (U.S. Burean of the Census, 1971b: Tables 21–22).

These facts are significant for our study because, as we show below, almost all of our married graduates are part of husband-wife (as distinguished from female-headed) families, just over half of our graduates are age 35 and under, and almost 50 percent of the black graduates' wives work full time. Hence the decline should be evident for our graduates in a small, family-income gap.[2]

Another fact significant for our study: It is not true that the lower the husband's income, the more a working wife contributes to family income. For the whole population, the "largest average income of wives and the largest labor-force participation rates are found for those of intermediate status with respect to education and husband's income" (Carter and Glick, 1970:211). Thus the largest incomes are *not* earned by the wives whose husbands earn the lowest incomes. This finding holds even more strongly for nonwhite than for white families. The median incomes of working black wives aged 25 to 44 rose as their husbands' incomes rose; the rise was very sharp in the range between no income and $6000 annually and more gradual after that point, dropping only after the husband's salary amounted to more than $15,000 annually. In contrast, median incomes of white working wives declined steadily as their husbands' incomes rose above the $4000 to $4999 level, and were lower than the median income for black wives whose husbands earned $5000 or more annually (Carter and Glick, 1970).

Thus the resulting difference in median incomes of black (as opposed to white) wives is greatest for those whose husbands earn incomes about equal to the average income of our various groups of college graduates. This situation is tempered somewhat by the additional fact that the median income of black wives was at most no more than 25 percent of their husbands' incomes. However, we would still expect that the wives of our black graduates would work more frequently than the wives of white graduates and, when working, contribute more to their families' incomes than would white graduates' wives. This situation should cause the family-income gap to be smaller than the personal-income gap. It may even be that black family incomes are greater than white family incomes in at least some of our matched samples because of (1) the much greater median incomes of working black wives whose husbands earn around $10,000 a year, and (2) the increasingly greater incomes of black women with some college education.

The key question for analysis are thus: (1) What proportion of the differences in family income result simply from the different proportions of black (versus white) wives who work? (2) Can we explain the greater proportion of black wives who work? (3) Which wives contribute more to family income as their income-producing resources increase (e.g., does an additional year of education bring more additional income to white or to black wives?).

GRADUATES' FAMILIES: A PROFILE

We first examine some of the graduates' characteristics that relate to this chapter's analysis. Table 5.1 shows that of those interviewed, at least 86 percent of the white graduates and between 75 and 83 percent of the black graduates were then married (that is, roughly 5 percent more white than black graduates are married). For all graduates, the differences between white and black family incomes are indeed less than the personal income differences (the former range between 30 and 55 percent of the differences in personal incomes). For married graduates, average personal and family incomes were slightly higher than for all graduates interviewed. The differences between married whites' and blacks' average personal incomes were comparable to those among all graduates; in addition, as we might expect from the above discussion, their differences in average family incomes were much less than the differences for all graduates. Indeed, the average family income of Frazier–2

TABLE 5.1   CHARACTERISTICS OF GRADUATES' FAMILIES

Characteristics	ASU Whites	ASU Blacks	MSU Whites	MSU Blacks	Frazier −1 Blacks	Frazier −2 Blacks
All graduates[a]						
Marital state (%)						
Married	86	75	88	79	83	78
Single	11	20	12	11	16	17
Divorced	2	0	0	5	2	2
Separated	0	4	0	3	0	2
Mean income[b]						
Personal	12,011	10,217	11,459	10,304	9,642	10,349
Family	13,574	12,925	13,060	12,451	12,573	12,718
Married graduates						
Mean income[b]						
Personal	12,696	10,996	11,933	10,800	10,139	10,943
Family	13,975	13,724	13,405	13,248	13,195	13,689
Working wives (%)						
Full time	23	48	15	40	49	49
Full and part time combined	30	55	24	50	62	55
Wife's mean						
Education	13.5	15.1	13.7	14.1	14.8	14.5
Father's education	10.7	10.0	10.4	10.0	11.4	11.2
Father's job status	45.4	26.5	41.2	26.2	34.2	35.7
Role	2.3	2.7	2.3	2.2	2.3	2.4
Mean number of children	2.3	1.97	2.23	2.21	1.96	1.98
Mean age at marriage	25.2	25.1	25.5	26.1	25.9	25.4
N	109	95	136	123	105	117

[a] For N's, see Table 2.1.
[b] As of 1966; adjusted in terms of 1957–59 dollars.

graduates (black) exceeded that of the white MSU graduates to which they were matched.

Considerably more black than white wives work. Between 55 and 62 percent of the black graduates' wives, but only 24 to 30 percent of the white wives, worked either full or part time.

Wives of black graduates tended to have slightly more education than wives of white graduates, though on the average, both sets of wives had at least some college education. The fathers of the white graduates' wives had about 10.5 years of education (about half a year more than those of ASU and MSU black graduates). The fathers of Frazier graduates' wives had more than 11 years of education, the most of any group of wives' fathers.

The fathers of white graduates' wives had the highest job status, on the average, followed by the fathers of Frazier graduates' wives. Fathers of black ASU and MSU graduates' wives had the lowest. It is interesting to note that the average job status of the fathers of graduates' wives parallels quite closely that of the graduates' fathers. Black and white married graduates show virtually no difference in the husband's conceptions of the wife's role, though black husbands from ASU held slightly less traditional views of this role than did other graduates.[3]

Finally, there was virtually no black-white difference in the mean number of children born to married graduates. That figure averages about two children per family. This figure is more meaningful when we recall that the age distributions for each school's samples of matched graduates are approximately the same; in addition, the average age at marriage for all sample members was the same—25 years. Thus each group of married graduates has had about the same length of time in which to bear children.

With the above characteristics established, we can now begin analysis that will answer the key question listed above. The first step is to establish the relationship between marriage and income. Subsequently we can examine the determinants of family income.

ANALYSIS

MARRIAGE AND PERSONAL INCOME

Common sense suggests that the higher family incomes of married graduates primarily reflect the financial contributions of working wives. Yet the above data showing married graduates' higher personal incomes, together with Farley and Hermalin's finding (1971), indicate that marriage itself is associated with higher personal income. Some might argue that the additional responsibilities of marriage induce an extra earning effort by husbands, resulting in higher average personal incomes for married men. Equally likely, however, is a subtler mechanism of self-selection: men in better jobs, making more money, have a slightly greater tendency to marry than other men (hence the observed relationship). One possible objection to this latter suggestion is that a larger (although still small) proportion of younger than older men are unmarried. Obviously, then, a more detailed analysis of the impact of marriage should control for age.

Table 5.2 shows the income value of marriage together with the income values of the four independent variables analyzed in Chapter 4. It also shows the *relative* effect of marriage, job status, and so on when the other variables are controlled. The income-value section shows that for ASU white and black graduates and MSU white graduates, being married rather than single sometimes results in sizable (average) additional personal income. For example, the coefficient for ASU blacks—2.54, or $2540—shows the average effect of marriage on the personal incomes of black ASU graduates, when the other four variables are controlled. The table seems to indicate a "high cost of remaining single," but this paradoxical result is seriously undercut by the likelihood of self-selection (suggested above). Unlike the less educated man who seeks additional income from additional education, the single man cannot, if self-selection holds, contemplate receiving financial benefits merely by getting married. One further point: In all four comparisons, married white graduates realized more additional personal income than the black graduates to whom they are matched.

The analysis of relative effects indicates that being married is fairly unimportant to personal income. For ASU white graduates, the effect of marriage on income parallels that of employment sector (only the third-ranked influence on income; see Table 5.2). Among ASU blacks it is as important as years of experience (the second-ranked factor). For the remaining groups, it ranks with the least important of the four factors previously analyzed.

DETERMINANTS OF FAMILY INCOME

We now examine the graduates' family incomes. One possible model for this analysis would begin with the model used to explain the determination of personal income and add to it. A graduate's personal income would certainly be the most important determinant of his family's income (given American families' almost universal adherence to the traditional division of labor). Another obvious factor should be whether the wife works.[4] Also of interest should be the factors that determine whether a wife works. For example, what is the relationship between her education and her employment status? Are the better- or the less-educated wives of college graduates more often employed? Perhaps education makes little difference: There may be little variation in the amount of wives' education because they have married college graduates, and

TABLE 5.2 INCOME VALUE AND RELATIVE EFFECTS, BY SAMPLE, OF FIVE INDEPENDENT VARIABLES

Independent Variables	ASU Whites	ASU Blacks	Frazier-1 Blacks	MSU Whites	MSU Blacks	Frazier-2 Blacks
Income value (unstandardized coefficients)						
Current-job status	.16[a]	.04	.07	.06	.10	.13
Graduate education	.55	.20	.96	.43	.37*	.56
Years of experience	.50	.16	.20	.30	.21	.39
Employment sector	3.61	3.12	2.59	3.62	.80	2.26*
Marriage[b]	5.08	2.54	.60	2.24*	1.08	1.47
Relative effects (standardized coefficients)						
Current-job status	.26	.10	.14	.12	.30	.22
Graduate education	.10	.07	.29	.10	.14*	.18
Years of experience	.43	.22	.24	.30	.29	.31
Employment sector	.19	.29	.18	.28	.07	.14*
Marriage	.21	.21	.04	.12*	.10	.08
Residual	(.80)	(.87)	(.80)	(.85)	(.83)	(.83)
N	126	127	127	155	155	149

[a] Underlined numbers are significant at $< .05$; numbers indicated by asterisks, at $.10 > p > .05$.

[b] Graduates were coded 1 if married; 0 if single, divorced, or separated.

men tend to marry women with educational attainments similar to their own. Wife's age is also likely to influence the probability of her working. To avoid analytic difficulties with this variable,[5] we used a variable—husband's years of experience—that was likely to correlate highly with wife's age.

Finally, if current social concern with traditional and nontraditional sex roles is at all indicative, the husband's conception of his wife's proper role in the family ought to affect whether she works. This factor should be less important when economic necessity pushes both spouses into the marketplace, but it *is* plausible for college graduates. The obvious hypothesis is that the more nontraditional a husband's conception, the greater the probability that his wife is employed.

A model using these elements is shown in Figure 5.1. It may be flawed in its omission of such characteristics of wives as their fathers' educational levels or job statuses; however, others have shown that such characteristics cannot compete with the influence of a man's characteristics on his wife's job status and income (see Blau and Duncan, 1967:342–343). These results are explained by the modest-to-high correlations between characteristics of wives' and husbands' families, wives' and husbands' characteristics, and the greater influence of characteristics of the husband and his family.

To begin analyzing this model, we first consider the personal-income coefficients in Table 5.3. If we compare these figures with corresponding figures in Table 4.1 (all graduates), we see that few of these relationships depend to any extent on whether the graduate is married. Job status has virtually the same personal-income value for married graduates as for all graduates. Likewise, except for Frazier–2 graduates, graduate education and years of experience have virtually the same impact on married as on all graduates.[6]

We now consider the effects of graduates' income, wives' education, and so forth on the probability of a wife's working full time. The dependent variable is dichotomous (wives working full time were coded 1; all others, 0).[7] The analysis shows that for all samples, an additional thousand dollars of a graduate's personal income reduced the probability of his wife's working by an amount ranging from zero to .02. For all but one sample, years of experience does not affect the probability of a wife's working full time. (For ASU white graduates, a difference of 10 years of experience corresponded to an increment of .2 in the probability that their wives worked full time.) For four samples of graduates, each additional year of wife's education increased the probability of her working from between .04 to .07. Finally, for three groups, the wives of less traditional husbands were more likely to be working full time. (A difference of one point on our index increased the probability of the wife's

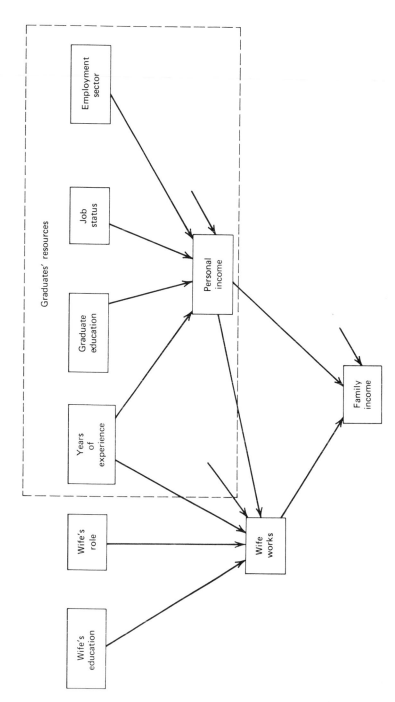

Figure 5.1   Model for the determination of family income.

Graduates' resources

Employment sector

Job status

Graduate education

Years of experience

Wife's role

Wife's education

Personal income

Wife works

Family income

TABLE 5.3 PERSONAL-INCOME VALUE, PROBABILITY VALUE OF WIFE'S WORKING, AND FAMILY-INCOME VALUE, BY SAMPLE, OF SEVERAL VARIABLES (CONSTRUCTED USING UNSTANDARDIZED REGRESSION COEFFICIENTS)

Variables	ASU Whites	ASU Blacks	Frazier-1 Blacks	MSU Whites	MSU Blacks	Frazier-2 Blacks
Personal-income value						
Current-job status	.15[a]	.05	.07	.04	.11	.12*
Graduate education	.76	.36	1.02	.41	.35	.50
Years of experience	.50	.20	.20	.30	.19	.50
Employment sector	3.39	2.19	2.79	4.12	.94	3.73
Probability of wife working (full time)						
Personal income	−.02	.00	−.02	−.01	−.02	−.02
Years of experience	.02	.00	.00	.01	.01*	.01*
Wife's education	.05	.03	.05	.01	.07	.04
Wife's role	.02	−.02	.11	.08	.01	.10
Family-income value						
Personal income	.97	.96	1.03	.94	1.09	.94
Wife working	3.70	4.66	4.20	4.34	4.64	3.09
N	109	95	105	136	123	117

[a] Underlined numbers were significant at $<.05$; numbers indicated by asterisks, at $.10 > p > .05$.

working by about .10.) In sum, wives of graduates are more likely to work (1) the less their husbands' personal incomes, (2) the higher their own educational levels, and (3) the less traditional their husband's conception of their proper role.

The last panel of Table 5.3 shows the family-income value of a working wife, taking the husband's personal income into account. The working wife's family-income value ranges from an average of just over $3000 (for Frazier-2 graduates) to $4550 (for ASU and MSU black graduates).

COMPONENT ANALYSIS

Table 5.1 shows large differences (around 25 percent) in the respective percentages of black and white wives who work (the black percentages are higher). We now want to explain these differences. We have just seen that the probability of wives' working is inversely proportional to the size of their husbands' income, and we can recall that black graduates' average personal income is less than that of white graduates. Our previous analysis showed that graduates' personal income can modestly affect a wife's probability of working. However, it is not the only variable with explanatory potential. We should also consider the effect of black versus white wives' relative amounts of education. In addition, it may simply be that black graduates' wives are more likely to work than white graduates' wives, even after differences in average personal income, education of wives, and so on have all been taken into account. We therefore analyzed the various components of the percentage difference in the probability of white versus black graduates' wives working full time.

For all groups of graduates, Table 5.4 shows, first, that from 3 to 6 points of the actual difference (roughly 25 percentage points) can be attributed to the greater average education of the black wives (that is, the higher their educational level, the more likely they were to work). Second, another 5 points in the difference can be attributed to the lower average personal income of the black husbands (given that regardless of race, the probability of wives' working varied inversely with the size of their husbands' incomes). Third, even after all other factors had been controlled, black wives were still more likely than white wives to work full time. This component, which may represent a racial factor, accounted for between 10 and 19 percentage points in three of the matched groups. It reached a hefty 40 points for ASU white and black graduates. However, as the total differences show, this figure was partly offset by other, positive components. Interestingly, differences in husbands'

TABLE 5.4 COMPONENTS OF DIFFERENCES IN THE PROPORTIONS OF BLACK AND WHITE GRADUATES' WIVES WORKING FULL TIME[a]

Components Reflecting	ASU Whites ASU Blacks	ASU Whites Frazier–1 Blacks	MSU Whites MSU Blacks	MSU Whites Frazier–2 Blacks
A. Differences in mean				
Personal income	−.005	−.046	−.022	−.022
Years of experience	.001	.002	.000	.008
Wife's education	−.053	−.060	−.027	−.031
Wife's role	.009	−.006	.001	−.001
Subtotal of A	−.048	−.114	−.048	−.046
B. Differences in the probability of working per				
Personal income	−.092	.023	.083	.097
Years of experience	.194	.140	−.049	−.062
Wife's education	.049	−.004	−.224	−.123
Wife's role	.051	−.114	.091	−.033
Subtotal of B	.202	−.045	−.099	−.121
C. Other (including racial) differences	−.400	−.193	−.104	−.162
Sum	−.246	−.262	−.251	−.329
Actual difference	−.245	−.261	−.251	−.333
Rounding error	−.001	.001	.000	.004

[a] Ten years of wife's education, $5000 in personal income, zero years of experience, and a score of 1 on husband's conception of his wife's role were used as the zero points in this analysis.

average years of experience and conceptions of the wife's proper role contributed nothing to explaining the greater likelihood of black wives working.

The remaining findings showed some differences between the ASU group (the matched white and black ASU graduates and Frazier–1 graduates) in contrast to the MSU group (white and black MSU graduates and Frazier–2 graduates). In the ASU group, black wives worked in inverse proportion to the amount of their husbands' years of experience (14 to 19 percentage points). It was less true of ASU black than white wives that the greater their education, the more likely they were to work; this subcomponent amounted to 5 points of the total percentage difference between groups of wives. In contrast, the corresponding subcomponents for the MSU group increased the difference in the proportions of working wives.

We next examine differences in the average family incomes of married black and white graduates. The average personal-income gap, favoring whites, should contribute to a family-income gap also favoring whites, but this component should be offset by the larger proportion of working black wives. The question, then, is whether these factors exactly offset each other. For all but the last matched group (see Table 5.5), the greater proportion of black working wives is not sufficient to offset the differences in black and white mean personal incomes. For MSU white and Frazier–2 graduates, though, the higher proportion of black working wives slightly more than offset the husbands' lower average personal incomes. The working wives of ASU black and Frazier–1 graduates added a little more to family income (from $117 to $226) than did the wives of white ASU graduates.[8] However, the working wives of white MSU graduates contributed slightly more than those of Frazier–2 graduates. The contribution of all other differences to overall family-income differences varies considerably by matched group; for three, the gap is narrowed by anywhere from a few dollars to $645, while for MSU graduates the gap is enlarged by a modest $134.

In sum, the largest positive contribution to average family-income differences is made by differences in husbands' average personal incomes, but this contribution (which favors white graduates) is largely negated by combinations of other subcomponents that vary by matched groups. The largest of these subcomponents is the greater proportion of black wives who work.

SUMMARY

Consistent with our expectations, we found that black graduates' wives work full time more often than do white graduates' wives. Furthermore, the family-income gap for white and black graduates was somewhat narrower than the gap between their personal incomes. Other principal findings were:

1. Married graduates from the two white samples and one of the four black groups of graduates had noticeably higher personal incomes than other graduates; as a partial result, white graduates in general also

TABLE 5.5　COMPONENTS OF DIFFERENCES IN THE AVERAGE FAMILY INCOMES OF BLACK AND WHITE MARRIED GRADUATES[a]

Components Reflecting	ASU Whites ASU Blacks	ASU Whites Frazier-1 Blacks	MSU Whites MSU Blacks	MSU Whites Frazier-2 Blacks
A. Differences in mean				
Personal income[a]	1.620	2.640	1.230	.932
Proportion of working wives	−1.140	−1.100	−1.160	−1.030
Subtotal of A	.480	1.540	.070	−.098
B. Differences in the effect on family income of proportion of working wives	−.226	−.117	−.046	.192
C. Other (including racial) differences	−.013	−.645	.134	−.377
Sum	.241	.778	.158	−.283
Actual differences	.251	.780	.157	−.284
Rounding error	.010	.002	.001	.001

[a] Family-income value of personal income is 1.000; see note 8 to this chapter.

　　realized more additional income when married than did married black graduates.

2.　The lower their husbands' incomes, the more likely wives were to work.

3.　A small but consistent portion of the larger percentage of working black wives could be attributed to their higher average educational levels and their husbands' lower average personal incomes. However, groups of matched graduates differed regarding the effect of husbands' years of experience on whether black wives were more or less likely to work.

4.　In general, the higher the graduates' wives' educational level, the more likely they were to work, regardless of race.

5.　The most sizable component of the larger percentage of black working wives appeared to be a racial factor: black wives either seek employment more often than white wives and/or receive acceptable employment more often than white wives simply because they are black.

6. Finally (as we expected from the national data cited early in this chapter), a component analysis of average family-income differences showed that the larger proportion of black wives who work full time did much to offset the effect of the white husbands' greater average personal incomes.

We should note the possibility (suggested by 1960 Census data) that the difference in the proportion of black and white women who work may be diminishing. While increasing proportions of married (or, at least, nonsingle) women, black and white, entered the labor force between 1940 and 1960, nonsingle white women did so to a noticeably greater degree. For married women living with their husbands, the difference in labor force participation rates of women 14 years old and over, for blacks (27 percent) and whites (12 percent) was 15 percent in 1940, and 10 percent (40 percent of blacks, 30 percent of whites) as of 1960 (Carter and Glick, 1970:173.).

Barring a diminution in the average personal-income differences for black and white married men, this shift in labor force participation could foreshadow a modest *increase* in the gap between blacks' and whites' family incomes. Further research into this possibility will require component analysis of more recent family-income data. If this trend applies equally to the wives of college-educated men, it surely signals a modest increase in the family-income gap since, as we have seen, the larger proportion of working black wives was the crucial factor offsetting the personal-income advantage of white graduates.

NOTES

1. We assume, both here and in our sample, that all wives of black graduates were black; all wives of white graduates, white.

2. We cannot directly prove the decline because our data do not extend over the last 10 years.

3. "Wife's role" is an index that runs from 1 to 4. Low values correspond to traditional conceptions of the woman's sex role; high values, to nontraditional conceptions. The graduates were asked: "Which *one* of the following statements comes closest to your opinion regarding the proper role of the adult woman in American society?" Respondents were then handed a card reading:

A. Her activities should be generally confined to the home and family—1.
B. She should divide her responsibilities between home and outside work only after her children are of school age—2.
C. She should divide her responsibilities between home and outside work, no matter how old her children are—3.
D. She should be allowed to choose to be entirely free of domestic responsibilities in order to work on an equal footing with men at all occupational levels—4.

4. Had we measures of wives' incomes, we could consider that factor also. Lacking this measure,

we have considered the direct effect on family income of the wife's working, controlling only for the effect of the husband's personal income.

5.   Including both wife's age and husband's years of experience in the same regression analysis would have caused serious problems, because these independent variables were too highly correlated.

6.   These and the previously noted differences for all, in contrast to married, graduates are unsystematic and fairly infrequent; we have therefore not attempted to explain them. Married graduates obviously constitute a high proportion of all graduates, and any other result would have been astounding. Separate estimates of the personal-income value of the four independent variables for the unmarried graduates might well be different. However, there were too few such graduates to permit separate analysis.

7.   We have bypassed the difficulties that can affect regressions on dichotomous, dependent variables (the absence of homoscedasticity in such variables can affect interpretation of the statistical significance of regression coefficients, and the usual designations of significance cannot be accepted at face value). Ashenfelter (1969) has shown that there is no a priori reason to expect the significance levels to be either liberally or conservatively estimated. In any event, our dichotomous dependent variables pose no problems for the interpretation of the coefficients themselves nor for our component analysis of differences in the proportions of working wives.

8.   We would expect the family-income value of personal income to be exactly 1.000, that is, each dollar of personal income would add exactly one dollar to family income. Estimates of this coefficient need not exactly coincide with this hypothesized value, but the analysis shows no significant difference (with one exception—Frazier-2 graduates) between the estimates and that value. For the purposes of a component analysis of average, family-income differences, we have substituted the values of 1.000 for each of the coefficients shown in Table 5.3. Hence there is no B subcomponent for personal incomes in Table 5.5.

6

RACE, CLASS, AND
SOCIAL PARTICIPATION

Earlier chapters have focused on black and white graduates' experiences in the marketplace. We therefore analyzed the relative impact of race and certain resources, such as education and job status, on such rewards as personal and family income.

This chapter examines selected aspects of graduates' organizational affiliations and life styles that have little to do with economic pursuits. We begin by analyzing graduates' satisfaction with their jobs and social activities. We look next at the organization a graduate feels is the most important he belongs to, and see how active he is in it and what type of organization it is. We then consider the frequency of certain varieties of religious, political, and cultural activity, and of visits with friends. Graduates' housing—rental versus ownership; rental cost or value of home owned; and, for black graduates, the actual versus preferred location of housing—is examined next. Finally, we consider graduates' preferences for various methods of achieving civil rights.

The goal of this analysis was to determine the differences, if any, in graduates' life styles and organizational affiliations, and the degree to which these differences were produced by racial and social class differences. Since these graduates had similar levels of education and similar social class backgrounds, and since some were graduates of the same schools in the same years, we might expect them to have rather similar life styles, and affiliations. In a wider sample of men with all levels of education, we would ordinarily expect racial and social-class differences to produce corresponding differences in life styles and organizational activities. And despite the restrictions we might expect from the limited ranges, and hence variations, in our graduates' incomes and educational levels, we may still observe such differences in this sample. The question then will be whether the racial or the social-class difference produces the greater differences in affiliations and in life styles.

Most previous research on this question has been devoted to the effects of race and social class on the "social participation" of men. Such participation has usually meant the number of organizational memberships held by a person, his level of activity in such organizations, or his membership and involvement in particular types of organizations, such as churches and unions. We examined somewhat broader, more varied activities than those previously considered, and our attitude and housing variables have not previously been treated as aspects of social participation. Nonetheless, previous research suggested some hypotheses that we tested.

Research into the effect of social class on social participation has usually found that a person's membership in voluntary associations and organizational activity increases as education and/or income increases (Lenski, 1956; Orum, 1966; Hodge and Treiman, 1968; Olsen, 1970). Axelrod (1956) offered an explanation: For professional and white-collar workers, social participation is often an extension of their formal work roles; hence the line dividing work from other activities is very hard to draw.

Studies of the effect of race on such activities have differed in their findings, procedures, and expectations. Some writers (Myrdal, cited in Rose, 1956:293–300), having observed that blacks are great joiners of organizations, term this behavior an almost pathological attempt to compensate lesser achievement in the marketplace with social recognition through black organizations. The findings of Babchuk and Thompson (1962) supported Myrdal's thinking. In addition, both Orum (1966) and Olsen (1970) found that a larger percentage of blacks than whites were active even when social class was controlled, and the differences were larger for those with lower status.[1] However, Olsen disputed the notion of pathological compensation because his data partly encompassed "public" activities such as cultural events, partisan political participation, and exposure to mass media that provide little or no escape from whites, much less compensation for their treatment of blacks. In addition, when Olsen examined by class the percentages holding organizational memberships (but not necessarily active ones), he found that blacks with lower socioeconomic status belonged more frequently than whites with such status. The reverse held for those with high socioeconomic status.

In sum, previous research shows that the individual level of social participation, variously measured, increases as social class rises, but researchers have
not discovered how the participation gap changes as class levels increase.
Hence the relative effects of race and social class on graduates' participation is
an empirically open question. Unlike our study, none of the previous research
was confined to a sample of college graduates.

VARIABLES AND PROCEDURE

VARIABLES

The variables used in this analysis, together with their measures, are as
follows.[2]

Satisfaction with Job. Graduates were asked (following Form and Geschwender, 1962:230): "How do you feel about your present job—would you say
it is very good (coded 5), pretty good, average, not too good, not good at all
(coded 1)?"

Most Satisfying Activity. Graduates were handed a card containing a list of
activities: recreational activities; participation in activities directed toward national or international betterment; career or occupational activities; re-
ligiously-oriented activities; family activities; participation as a citizen in affairs of the community; other. They were then asked "Which *one* of the
activities on this card has given you the *most* satisfaction in your life?"[3] We
divided the activities into two groups: activities usually pursued by graduates
primarily in their role as family members or marital partners (recreational
activities; religion and family activities), and those usually pursued by
graduates primarily in extrafamilial roles—either as members of occupations
or professions or in their role as citizens of a community or country (activities
directed toward national or international betterment; career or occupational
activities; participation in community affairs). We coded graduates 1 on this
variable if their most satisfying activity was from the first group; 0, if from the
second.[4]

Level of Activity in the Most Important Organization Belonged To. We
asked graduates: "Do you belong to any organizations—like professional,

social, church organizations or other organizations?"[5] We then asked those belonging to any organizations to list them in order of their importance to the respondent, and to indicate whether they were "very active," "fairly active," or "not active at all" in each organization listed.[6]

Type of Organization in Which the Graduate is Most Active. These were classified as follows: civil rights; religious, nationalist, fraternal, service, cultural, or educational; political or civic; professional or business; patriotic or veteran's; and others. We grouped these broadly under two headings: those concerned with politics, civic affairs, and/or civil rights (coded 1), and all others (coded 0).

Religious Activity. We asked graduates: "How often do you attend religious services—once a week or more, two or three times a month, once a month, or less often than that?" The first answer was coded 5; the last, 2. Those who said "never" were coded 1.

Political Activity. We asked graduates: "During the last year, have you engaged in any of the following activities—signed a petition for or against some legislation; written a letter or sent a telegram to a public official; collected money for a political cause or group; or contributed money for a political cause or group?" Participation in one or more such activities was coded 1; no activity, 0.

Cultural Activity. Graduates were asked: "During the last six months, altogether, how often have you gone to a museum, concert, or play?" The response categories were: never, once, twice, 3, 4, 5, 10, 11 to 19, and 20 or more times; these were coded from 0 ("never") to 7.

Visiting Friends. Graduates were asked: "During an average month, how many times do you get together with friends in the evening or on the weekend?" Zero to 6 times a month were coded 0 to 6, respectively; a 7 was assigned to those who visited 7 or more times a month. If the graduate was married and living in the same household with his wife, he was also asked: "Do you usually get together with friends alone, or does it usually include your wife?" "Alone, without wife," was coded 1; "with wife," 3; "about equally," 2.

Ownership of Housing. Respondents were asked if they owned or rented the house in which they were living. Owners were coded 1; renters, 0.

Average Rent or Value of Housing. Owners were asked: "How much would it be worth if you were to sell . . . your home?" Those who rented were asked: "How much rent per month do you pay?" The value of houses owned was coded in terms of hundreds of dollars.

Actual and Preferred Location of Black Graduates' Housing. Black graduates were asked about their actual and preferred racial compositions for their neighborhoods. Categories and codes used to describe neighborhoods were: "all Negro," 1; "integrated but mostly Negro" or "mostly Negro," 2; "half Negro and half white," 3; and "mostly white," 4. They were also asked if they had ever attempted to purchase housing in white neighborhoods and, if so, whether they had been successful.

Respondent's Support for Civil Rights Methods. Hoping to illuminate the continuing controversy over appropriate methods for achieving civil rights, we asked respondents to tell us whether they agreed or disagreed with each of the following methods of achieving civil rights: rent strikes; integrating schools through involuntary busing of children; violent demonstration; lobbying for legislation; forcing work stoppages on construction projects; and nonviolent protest demonstrations. Lobbying for legislation was dropped from analysis because few disagreed with it. Affirmative responses were coded 1; responses indicating disagreement, 0.

PROCEDURE

When analyzing the effect of race and social class on our various measures of social participation, we used each graduate's personal income to indicate his social class. The effects of graduate education, years of experience, and employment sector were considered only peripherally; our primary intent was to control for their influence while focusing on the effects of class and race.[7]

To examine the effects of race, we first compared the average levels of social participation of white and black graduates. We then considered the significant effects of social class on this form of participation by regressing participation on income as well as graduate education, years of experience, and employment sector, *within* groups of white and black graduates.[8] We also took a close look at the effects of race on each type of participation when social class (personal income), graduate education, years of experience, and employment sector are controlled. This effect of race is assessed by a method that is simpler and less detailed than the regression standardization used earlier. We simply combined matched white and black samples, and regressed type of social participation on the four factors[9] and on race (1 = white; 0 = black).[10]

ANALYSIS

In this discussion, the line numbers in the text correspond to the noneconomic variables as listed in the tables.

ORGANIZATIONAL PARTICIPATION

Job Satisfaction. Previous research has shown that current-job satisfaction rises as social class rises (see Form and Geschwender, 1962, who also found, interestingly, that educational level was *not* related to job satisfaction). Line 1 of Table 6.1 shows that, on the average, ASU whites are more satisfied with their jobs than are ASU blacks or Frazier–1 blacks; similarly, MSU whites are more satisfied than MSU blacks. However, MSU whites were less satisfied than Frazier–2 graduates. For three of four matched samples, then, white graduates were more satisfied than blacks with their jobs.

If the usual hypothesis holds, satisfaction should rise with personal income. Line 1 or Table 6.2 supports this hypothesis, but only modestly. For ASU whites, an increase of $1000 in income corresponds to an increase of .02 in satisfaction (where satisfaction is scaled from 1 to 5). A difference of 1 on the scale corresponds to the difference between feeling "pretty good" and "average" about present jobs. A difference of $10,000 would correspond to .2 on this scale. Although statistically significant,[11] this enormous difference in personal incomes corresponds to only a very modest difference in average satisfaction. For MSU blacks, though, $10,000 corresponds to a more substantial difference—0.5 on this scale.

For all samples, graduate education, years of experience, and employment sector had an insignificant and insubstantial effect of job satisfaction; we thus omitted these coefficients from Table 6.2.

Line 1 of Table 6.3 shows the effect of race on job satisfaction when other factors are controlled. In the ASU group, white graduates are significantly more satisfied than black graduates; the same does not hold in the MSU group. Regarding the relative effect of race and personal income with all relevant factors controlled, we find that for ASU white and black graduates, it would take roughly $9000 difference in personal income to produce a social-participation difference equal to the white-black participation difference. A difference of roughly $4000 would produce the same difference in social participation as that observed between MSU whites and blacks.

We considered race and personal income to have equal impact on our measure of social participation *if* a difference of $5000 in personal income corresponded to the same difference in social participation level as did the difference between being a white, in contrast to black, graduate. If it required a larger personal-income difference to produce a social-participation difference equal to the difference made by race, we concluded that race was the more important factor. If the reverse, then personal income was judged more important.[12] Using this convention, we concluded that for graduates in the ASU group, race had more influence than class on job satisfaction. The reverse held for the MSU group. In short, neither race nor class had a consistently stronger influence.

Most Satisfying Activity. Our question here was whether black graduates or white, with higher incomes or lower, were more likely to find greater satisfaction in familial rather than extrafamilial activities. Line 2 of Table 6.1 shows that the proportions of white graduates listing family, religious, or recreational activities as their most satisfying is higher than the corresponding proportions of black graduates. The difference is greater when we compare ASU whites with their black classmates, and MSU whites with *their* classmates.

Line 2 of Table 6.2 shows that the higher-income graduates had a greater preference for extrafamilial activities than graduates with less income. This relationship was significant only for MSU blacks, and even then was very modest. For MSU blacks, income differences of $5000 corresponded to an additional 10 percent probability of finding extrafamilial activities more satisfying. In addition, the MSU blacks who completed additional education were even more likely to find extrafamilial activities their most satisfying outlet. This coefficient was significant for only one individual sample, but for two matched samples, ASU white/Frazier–1 and MSU white/Frazier–2 graduates, the larger sample size produced significant negative relationships between graduate education and the more satisfying activity. The respective coefficients were −.03 and −.04. Thus an additional year of graduate education leading to a degree results in an additional 3 to 4 percent probability of finding extrafamilial activities more satisfying than familial activities.

When we consider the effect of race, taking personal income, graduate education, years of experience, and employment sector into account, we find it significant only for ASU whites and their black classmates, and for MSU whites and their black classmates (see line 2, Table 6.3). About 12 percent more whites than blacks find familial activities more satisfying. Even when personal income has a significant effect on this variable (one matched sample—MSU whites and blacks), a difference of $5000 in income cor-

TABLE 6.1 MEANS OF NONECONOMIC VARIABLES BY SAMPLES OF GRADUATES

Noneconomic Variables	ASU Group			MSU Group		
	ASU Whites	ASU Blacks	Frazier–1 Blacks	MSU Whites	MSU Blacks	Frazier–2 Blacks
1. Job satisfaction	4.39	4.15	4.08	4.37	4.23	4.47
2. Most satisfactory activity	.69	.56	.57	.67	.56	.62
3. Organizational activity	1.98	2.26	2.26	1.89	2.18	2.27
4. Type of organization	.08	.24	.12	.10	.16	.14
5. Religious activities						
Church attendance	3.49	3.16	3.37	3.45	3.63	3.23
Bible reading	2.30	2.99	2.95	2.70	3.36	3.09
Church responsibilities	.24	.24	.25	.28	.37	.29
6. Political activities						
Signed a petition	.45	.53	.44	.48	.48	.41
Wrote a letter	.37	.49	.48	.53	.43	.42
Collected money	.11	.17	.16	.07	.08	.12
Contributed money	.35	.48	.44	.34	.33	.48
7. Cultural activities						
Attendance	2.60	3.00	3.30	3.10	3.40	3.10
Books read	3.90	4.30	5.10	4.50	4.40	4.00
8. Visits with friends	3.44	3.43	3.64	3.73	3.37	3.44
9. Visits include wife	2.79	2.69	2.65	2.87	2.46	2.70
10. Home ownership	69%	60%	50%	85%	68%	64%
11. Rental value ($/month)	$125	112	113	154	93	114
12. Home value ($100 units)	315	234	220	224	172	196

13. Endorse civil rights methods

Nonviolent demonstrations	.93	.92	.84	.88	.87	.90
Rent strikes	.48	.81	.82	.54	.71	.86
Work stoppages	.25	.77	.74	.24	.60	.68
Busing	.12	.60	.48	.17	.52	.59
Violent demonstrations	.02	.25	.31	.03	.11	.28
N	127	126	127	155	155	149

TABLE 6.2 EFFECTS OF PERSONAL INCOME AND OTHER VARIABLES ON NONECONOMIC VARIABLES

Noneconomic Variables	Income-Producing Resource	ASU Group			MSU Group		
		Whites	Blacks	Frazier-1	Whites	Blacks	Frazier-2
1. Job satisfaction	Income	.02[a]	.03	.04	.02	.05	.01
2. Most satisfactory activity	Income	.00	-.01	-.01	-.01	-.02	.00
3. Organizational activity	Income	.02	-.02	.01	-.02	.01	-.01
	Graduate education	.00	.04	.03	-.03	-.01	.01
	Sector	.05	-.08	-.05	.17	-.02	-.21*
4. Type of organization	Income	.00	.02	.02	.01	-.00	.00
	Graduate education	-.01	.01	-.04	-.04	.00	.01
	Sector	.12	-.01	.00	.14	.07	-.06
5. Cultural activities							
Attendance	Income	.06	.03	.09	.04	-.04	-.02
	Graduate education	.17	.18	-.18	.02	-.02	.06
	Sector	-.30	.04	-.81*	-.38	-1.06	-.25
Books read	Income	.03	.08	-.02	.04	-.01	.05
	Graduate education	.04	.15	.17	.03	-.05	-.02
	Sector	-.37	-1.68	-1.59	-.79	-1.74	-.52
6. Visits with friends	Income	.06	-.01	-.02	.05	.00	.02
	Graduate education	.20	-.19	.14	.29	-.08	-.03
7. Visits include wife	Income	.01	-.01	.01	.00	.01	.01
	Graduate education	.00	-.08	-.02	-.08	-.04	.01
8. Home ownership	Income	.02	.01	.02	.01	.03	.01
	Years of experience	.01	.02	.02	.01	.01	.03
9. Rental value	Income	5.10*	2.20*	11.00	—[b]	4.70	3.70
10. Home value	Income	8.55*	5.35	7.32	7.89	7.86	3.57

[a] Underlined numbers were significant at $p < .05$; numbers indicated by asterisks, at $.10 > p > .05$.

[b] Analysis could not be run; see text for explanation.

TABLE 6.3 EFFECTS OF RACE ON NONECONOMIC VARIABLES IN MATCHED GROUPS OF GRADUATES, CONTROLLING FOR PERSONAL INCOME, GRADUATE EDUCATION, YEARS OF EXPERIENCE, AND EMPLOYMENT SECTOR

Noneconomic Variables	ASU Whites and		MSU Whites and	
	ASU Blacks	Frazier-1 Blacks	MSU Blacks	Frazier-2 Blacks
1. Job satisfaction	.27	.24*	.14	−.07
2. Most satisfactory activity	.12*	.07	.13	.03
3. Organizational activity	−.27	−.31	−.30	−.37
4. Type of organization	−.19	−.07	−.09	.07*
5. Religious activities				
Church attendance	.24	.20	−.14	.05
Bible reading	−.64	−.60	−.59	−.46
Church responsibilities	−.01	−.01	−.09	−.05
6. Political activities				
Signed a petition	−.08	.03	.02	.07
Wrote a letter	−.13	−.11	.11*	.12
Collected money	−.08*	−.06	−.02	−.04
Contributed money	−.17	−.15	.00	−.14
7. Cultural activities				
Attendance	−.39	−.61	−.25	.00
Books read	−.07	−.58*	.28	.41
8. Visits with friends	−.09	−.15	.44*	.36
9. Visits include wife	.17	.19	.38	.17
10. Home ownership	.02	.11	.16	.18
11. Rental value ($/month)	18.90*	19.40	48.30	36.40
12. House value ($100 units)	62.11	64.87	49.81	41.38
13. Endorse civil rights methods				
Nonviolent demonstrations	.01	.12	.01	.00
Rent strikes	−.31	−.29	−.16	−.29
Work stoppages	−.51	−.43	−.33	−.43
Busing	−.48	−.30	−.35	−.42
Violent demonstrations	−.23	−.27	−.08	−.26

[a] Underlined numbers are significant at $p < .05$; numbers indicated by asterisks, at $.10 > p > .05$.

responds to no more than a 5 percent greater likelihood that graduates with higher incomes will find extrafamilial activities more satisfying. This percentage is less than the effect of race on this sample. In short, for whites matched to black classmates at ASU or MSU, race has more influence than class on the probability that familial activities will prove more satisfying. For the other two matched samples, neither factor had a significant influence.

Level of Organizational Activity.   Much of the time that graduates are away from their jobs or families is spent working for various voluntary organizations. Because such a large percentage of our graduates belonged to at least one such organization, we wanted to investigate their level of activity in them. This variable is difficult to compare meaningfully when some respondents belong to one, and others to three or more, organizations. So for each graduate we examined only the level of activity in the organization that he had deemed most important.

Line 3 of Table 6.1 recalls Orum's first finding: black graduates display a higher average activity level. However, line 3 of Table 6.2 shows that neither personal income nor graduate education has a significant impact on the level of activity. When we consider the effects of race while controlling the four factors (line 3, Table 6.3), we still find that blacks are more active, on the average, than whites. The difference corresponds to one-third of the difference between scale values (for example, one-third of the distance between being very and fairly active). Race, then, has more influence than class on activity.

The effects of employment sector on activity level (line 3, Table 6.2) are also worth noting. While the relationship is significant for only one black sample, the pattern of nonsignificant coefficients suggests an interesting hypothesis for study elsewhere: of those working in the public sector, blacks are more active than whites; of those in the private, whites are more active.

Type of Organization.   Again working with most important organization, we examined the type of organization preferred by graduates: political/civic/civil rights organizations, or all others. Our questions were whether black or white graduates were more likely to list the first type of organization, and whether graduates with more income and graduate education were more likely to list this type as their most important membership.

As expected, line 4 of Table 6.1 shows higher proportions of black graduates electing political, civic, or civil rights organizations as most important. Table 6.2 (line 4) shows that for half the samples, the greater the personal income, the greater the probability of listing this type. For these three samples, a difference of $5000 would correspond to a difference of from 5 to 10 percent in this probability. Also, for two of the six groups, increasing graduate education decreased this same probability. Evidently, increasing amounts of education and income have different impacts on these graduates' commitments to political organizations. Line 4 of Table 6.3 shows that black graduates still elect political, civic, or civil rights organizations more frequently than white graduates; in addition, the effects of income and education, when statistically significant, are comparable to or slightly larger than the effect of race for all but one matched sample (ASU blacks and whites).[13]

These findings should be qualified in one respect. If we analyze the frequency of subtypes of political organizations, we find that black graduates listed civil rights organizations more frequently than the other two kinds. The differences just discussed, then, partly reflect differences in the probability of listing civil rights organizations as most important.

Religious Activity. We next examined several specific kinds of social participation, beginning with religious activity. We might expect black graduates to be more religiously active than white ones (Orum, 1966; Olsen, 1970). Certainly if blacks have traditionally found compensation anywhere for the discrimination they endured from whites, they have found it in religion (see Frazier, 1964). Yet this expectation may need qualification when social class if controlled. How much of black religiosity actually reflects differences in the average social class of blacks and whites? The literature on lower- and upper-class religiosity is not as consistent as our stereotypes of lower-class religiosity would have us believe (Demerath, 1965). We therefore chose to test the general hypothesis of the social participation literature: The higher a person's social class, the more likely he is to participate actively in an organization such as the church.

We examined three aspects of religious activity: church attendance, church responsibilities (for example, teaching Sunday school), and one activity not necessarily related to organized religious activity, Bible reading. Line 5, Table 6.1 shows that all groups of graduates attend church somewhere between once and two or three times a month. White graduates attend slightly more often than blacks in three of the four possible comparisons. The samples show virtually no differences in the proportion of graduates taking on various church responsibilities (the only notable finding: 37 percent of the MSU blacks assumed such responsibilities, roughly 7 percent more than the corresponding proportion of their white classmates). On average level of Bible reading, black graduates consistently exceed whites, but the average, absolute difference was modest at best.

When we examined the effect of social class, we found that graduate education and personal income virtually never influenced any of the religious variables significantly. We therefore did not display the figures in Table 6.2. In contrast, years of experience (also not shown in the table) significantly influenced church attendance and Bible reading in about half of the individual and matched samples. A difference of 10 years' experience corresponded to roughly a third of a unit on the scale of church attendance and roughly half a unit on the Bible-reading scale. In each instance the older graduates showed higher frequencies.

When we controlled for the four factors (line 5, Table 6.3), the only statistically significant impact of race was on Bible reading. On the Bible-reading scale, one unit corresponds to the difference between reading the Bible several times a month and once a month, or between reading the Bible almost never and several times a year. On this scale, blacks read the Bible roughly half a unit more than whites. Analysis of the other two religious-activity variables showed no significant differences between white and black graduates. In short, our data do not support the belief that black graduates find religion a compensation for the ills of the world.

Political Activity. Political organizations not primarily representing black interests have usually not attracted black participants. However, obstructions to voter registration and other restrictions on participation in the wider political life of this country have recently diminished. When he controlled for income, Orum (1966) found blacks more likely than whites to participate in political organizations; furthermore, when education was controlled, blacks proved to be just as likely to have voted in 1960. Orum viewed the latter finding as part of a positive shift in the nationwide voting turnout of Negroes.

Olsen (1970) found that with social class controlled, blacks scored higher than whites on six indexes of political participation: political organization participation, political discussion, registration, voting, partisan political activities, and government contracts (contacting government officials). He found the racial difference on the first index quite small. Unfortunately, his sample included only 27 blacks of above-average and high status combined, in contrast to 300 whites of comparable status levels. We therefore view his findings with caution. Taken together, Olsen's and Orum's work suggest that our black graduates will be just as politically active as our white graduates; with social class controlled, blacks may even prove the more active.

Line 6 of Table 6.1 shows the average proportion of graduates in each sample who engaged in four kinds of political activity during the year prior to sampling. First, as many as a third to a half reported having signed a petition, written a letter, or contributed money. There was no consistent racial differences in the proportions who signed petitions, but blacks tended to collect and contribute money more frequently than whites. ASU blacks and Frazier-1 blacks tended more often than ASU whites to write at least one letter, but MSU whites wrote more often than their matching black graduates.

Analysis of the effects of the four factors on these activities (not included in Table 6.2) showed that income and graduate education were generally insignificant. The exceptions: for nine of the individual cases examined (six samples times four kinds of activities) and about half of the matched samples, income significantly affected the probability of engaging in these activities: the greater the incomes, the greater that probability. When income was significant, a difference of $10,000 corresponded to a difference in this probability ranging from 7 to 29 percent, with 12 percent the rough average. Not surprisingly, the likelihood of contributing money was significantly affected by income in four of the nine individual samples. In addition, for three of the six samples, a difference of 3 years of graduate education corresponded to differences of between 12 and 18 percent in the probability of contributing money at least once.

With all other factors controlled (line 6, Table 6.3), we found that race still had the same effect on the probability of engaging in these political activities as the differences in averages (Table 6.1) had suggested. Race had no significant effect on the signing of petitions or, by and large, on the collecting of money. For three of four matched samples, a significantly larger proportion of blacks than whites contributed money. In two matched samples, more whites than blacks wrote at least one letter. In short, our findings are consistent with our interpretation of Orum's and Olsen's results: Black graduates are about as active politically as whites and perhaps a little more active than whites in collecting money.

LIFE STYLES

We now examine selected elements of the graduates' life styles: how often they attend cultural events and visit friends (with and without their wives), and what kinds of housing they choose.

Cultural Participation. Cultural participation is a likely element of college graduates' life style. Specifically, Olsen (1970) found that blacks participate slightly more than whites. Because attendance at plays and concerts can be expensive, we might expect graduates with larger incomes to attend more often. Finally, we would expect those with graduate degrees to read more books than graduates with B.A. degrees.

Line 7 of Table 6.1 shows that ASU blacks and Frazier–1 blacks attended cultural events a little more often, and read books a little more frequently, than did ASU whites; no similar patterns held for the MSU group. The expected impact of personal income materialized for only two groups (line 5, Table 6.2). A difference of $10,000 would correspond to roughly one more event attended each 6 months (.6 to .9 more). Graduate education did not significantly influence attendance, and neither income nor graduate education affected the number of books read.

Surprisingly, however, employment sector (line 7, Table 6.2) had noticeable effects. For four of the six samples, private-sector employees averaged from three-quarters to one and three-quarters fewer books during the immediately prior 6 months than did public-sector employees. A similar tendency, for public-sector employees to attend more cultural events, was significant in two samples. Apparently, then, public-sector employment encouraged the college educated to enjoy cultural pursuits. We can offer no strong explanation for this finding. Public-sector employment may simply tend to attract people with stronger cultural interests (that is, there may be no necessary link between public-sector employment per se and consumption of culture).

When all other factors were controlled (line 7, Table 6.3), in only one matched group did blacks attend significantly more cultural events and read more books than whites. Otherwise, there were generally no significant differences between the two racial groups; each attended an average of 6 concerts, plays, and so forth, and read 8 to 10 books during the immediately preceding year.

Visiting.   Like cultural participation, visiting with friends is a form of social participation that occurs largely outside of organizational membership. Olsen found that blacks scored higher than whites on a friends-interaction index, though the differences are suggestive at best for higher-status persons (the sample size was small). Beyond this finding and the general hypothesis (stated above) regarding the relation between class and social participation, we approached these data with no strong expectations.

Line 8 of Table 6.1 shows that members of all samples visited friends between three and four times a month. There is virtually no difference between blacks and whites in the ASU group; MSU whites visited a little more often than did MSU or Frazier–2 blacks. Line 6 of Table 6.2 shows that personal income had no consistent effect on visiting. Likewise, years of experience and employment sector were not significant. Graduate education, though, had a significant relationship to visiting. In three of the four comparisons, increased graduate education was associated with more visits by whites, but fewer by blacks. For example, an MSU white graduate with 3 more years of education than a white classmate visited with friends about once a month more (3 × .29 = .09) than the classmate. A black graduate in a comparable comparison made one visit less every 4 months (3 × −.08 = −.24). For MSU whites and blacks, then, the difference resulting from 3 additional years of graduate education came to a little more than one visit a month. These differences may indicate that these white and black graduates made and kept different numbers of friends, depending on how much graduate education they had had.

Finally, line 8 of Table 6.3 shows that even with graduate education, employment sector and other variables controlled, ASU whites visited friends a little less often than did ASU and Frazier–1 blacks; MSU whites did so more often than their black counterparts.

Seeking further insight into the graduates' life styles as expressed in visiting practices, we asked them if their wives typically went along on these visits. It is characteristically middle class for couples to go visiting together, and characteristically working class for spouses to go visiting alone. The inclusion or exclusion of the wife thus might prove a modest barometer of the class character of graduates' life styles.

Line 9 of Table 6.1 shows a modest tendency for whites to include their wives more often than blacks. However, for all groups of graduates, wives were included from 75 to 100 percent of the time. None of the four factors consistently influenced this variable (line 7, Table 6.2). For the ASU group, public-sector employees consistently included their wives significantly more often than did private-sector employees (this finding was virtually the only interesting one from this part of the analysis). With the four factors controlled, whites (especially MSU whites in contrast to the black classmates) included their wives more often than blacks (line 8, Table 6.3). Again translating the scale used into a percentage of the time that wives were included, we found that the racial difference corresponded to between 8 and 19 percent.

In short, we found only a modest difference in the frequency with which white and black graduates visited their friends, and a slightly greater preference by black graduates for all-male visiting. Thus the data confirm the primarily middle-class character of our graduates' visiting practices: despite slight differences, couples tend to do the visiting.

Housing. The decision to buy a home rather than rent a house or apartment has obvious implications for one's life style. While rented dwellings can be made to express one's personality and taste, ownership usually enables greater expression. Line 10 of Table 6.1 shows that a modestly greater proportion of white than black graduates (from 9 to 21 percent) owned rather than rented their homes. We expected that the wealthier and the older graduates would be more likely to own than rent, and the data supported this expectation (line 8, Table 6.2). Where significant for individual samples of graduates (a total of four), an additional $5000 in income raised the probability of ownership between 5 percent (for Frazier–1 blacks) and 15 percent (MSU blacks). The same relationship was significant for all four matched samples (the corresponding increments in probabilities ranged from 5 to 8 percent). Similarly, to a significant degree in three individual samples, older graduates owned more often than younger ones—5 years of experience corresponded to an additional 10 to 15 percent probability of buying a home. Graduate education and employment sector had no significant effect on any sample.

When we controlled these four factors (line 10, Table 6.3), we found no significant difference in the probability that whites or blacks in the ASU group would own homes; however, in the MSU group, significantly more whites than blacks (16 to 18 percent) owned rather than rented. In their frequently urban areas of residence (see line 13, Table 3.1 above), MSU blacks and Frazier–2 graduates either had less desire than whites to purchase housing, or there was less housing of requisite quality available for purchase by blacks, even when they had income, education, and employment experience, comparable to whites who had purchased homes. For the MSU group, race was clearly more important than income: It took much more than $5000 to produce the same difference in ownership percentage that the racial difference produced.

Average Rent/Housing Value. Differences in average rent or house value can indicate the combined influence of financial means, available housing, and life style. If we could assume no restrictions on house choice or supply for black graduates, we could statistically remove the effects of any life-style differences that result from housing investment. Unfortunately, we cannot.

Lines 11 and 12 of Table 6.1 show that whites spend more for rent, and own homes with greater estimated value, than do blacks. Rent differences range from $12 to $60 a month, running considerably larger for the MSU group. Lines 9 and 10 of Table 6.2 show that the higher the personal income, the greater the rent paid or housing value for every sample of graduates.[14] For all graduates, an additional $1000 of income corresponded to between $2 and

$11 more rent per month; an additional $5000, from $10 to $55 more. Likewise, an additional $5000 of income corresponded to anywhere from $1500 to better than $4000 (5 × 8.55) in housing value; however, for whites these dollar figures were systematically (but not significantly) larger. Apparently white graduates with increasing incomes bought moderately more expensive homes than blacks with comparable income, graduate education, and so forth.

Lines 10 and 11 in Table 6.3 show coefficients that represent the average difference in rent or house value of white and black graduates with the four factors, controlled. White graduates spent from $19 to $48 a month more than did black graduates in average rent, and owned homes worth $4138 to $6487 more. As a rough average of averages, then, we can say that blacks paid $30 less rent a month than did whites, and owned homes worth $4000 less. If we took a similar average of averages with respect to the effects of income on rent paid or house value, a difference of $5000 corresponded to differences of about $24 per month in rent and $3600 in housing value. In general, then, differences in rent and value due to race exceeded those due to class. One difference should be noted. For the ASU group, the differences by race in rent paid are smaller, and in home value larger, than the average difference made by $5000 additional income. Thus, for these two groups, class had more relative influence than race on renters, but much less relative influence than race on homeowners. For the MSU group, in partial contrast, differences by race in both rent and house value were larger than the average difference made by $5000 income. For these graduates, race had *more* influence than class on both renters and owners.

These figures suggest that white and black college graduates consume housing differently, but many questions remain unanswered. Do black graduates, in contrast to white graduates of comparable means, own less valuable homes and/or rent less expensive places because they choose to do so, or because better, more expensive housing is too difficult to obtain where blacks prefer to live? Regardless of the answer, differences as great as $40 a month in rent (the MSU group) and more than $6000 in house value (the ASU group) exist. Whether these differences are large enough to reflect notable differences in life style is open for discussion. Let us presume a figure for rent (per month) or for housing value that represents a threshold between life styles. To the extend that rent/home-value differences can convey life-style differences, anything greater than this threshold figure should represent a detectable life-style difference. This threshold figure should vary with the average rent or value of graduates' homes. In view of the ranges of rent ($100 to $150)

TABLE 6.4 BLACK GRADUATES' ACTUAL VERSUS PREFERRED
NEIGHBORHOODS: RACIAL COMPOSITION

	ASU Blacks	Frazier–1 Blacks	MSU Blacks	Frazier–2 Blacks
1. Mean actual composition	2.81	2.61	2.45	2.60
2. Mean preferred composition	3.50	3.32	3.17	3.16
3. Difference between mean actual and preferred composition	.69	.71	.72	.56
4. Percent of all				
Who tried to buy/rent in white areas	.75	.66	.58	.64
Who bought/rented in white areas	.52	.47	.43	.44
5. Percent successful who tried	.70	.71	.74	.69
6. Percent unsuccessful who cited racial bias	.39	.40	.66	.46

and house values ($16,000 to $32,000), $40 per month is probably slightly below a threshold difference for rent; likewise, a $5000 difference probably exceeds a house-value threshold.

By such arbitrary reasoning we could conclude that for renters, housing consumption is not affected by race. For homeowners the reverse is true, and this difference is accentuated by the fact that more whites than blacks own their own homes.

Blacks' Actual versus Preferred Locations. The findings just discussed may be illuminated if we examine blacks' actual versus their preferred housing locations. Current controversies over the expansion of integrated housing, and its concomitant implications for school assignments, make this subject an important one. The actual racial composition of the neighborhoods in which the black graduates lived (see Table 6.4) ranged, on the average, from mostly Negro to half Negro and half white. Of the four groups of black graduates, ASU blacks lived in neighborhoods with the most whites; MSU blacks, in neighborhoods with the least (line 1, Table 6.4). All groups of black graduates preferred housing in neighborhoods with greater percentages of whites (line 2, Table 6.4). (A rough translation of blacks' categorical answers into likely proportions of white residents suggests that the blacks prefer neighborhoods that are 50 to 75 percent white.[15]) The mean difference between actual and preferred composition (line 3) amounted to between 25 and 35 percent white. ASU blacks preferred higher white proportions (about 75 percent) than any other group.

We next examined the attempts made by some black graduates to buy homes in white areas (and, hence, presumably to move out of black areas, although that presumption is not logically necessary). Of all blacks in our sample, between 43 and 52 percent of each group had bought in white areas (section 4). From 58 to 75 percent of each sample had made the attempt (section 4). ASU blacks had tried most frequently; MSU blacks, least frequently. Of those who had tried, a rather uniform 70 percent had been successful (line 5). Because we wanted to know whether race had been a likely factor in the failure of some who had tried to rent or buy in white areas, we asked respondents to indicate the cause of their failure from a list of possible factors. Race was chosen by between 40 and 66 percent of the unsuccessful. MSU blacks cited race far more frequently than did the other groups, and while they were often successful if they had actually tried to buy or rent, a smaller percentage of this group (58 percent) tried than of any other group.

Support for Civil Rights Methods. Finally, we examined graduates' support (or lack of it) for various methods of achieving civil rights. The rationale of doing so is straightforward; these means have become the center of a controversy that formerly attached itself more to the goals themselves. Here, as before, we wanted to probe the relative effects of class (personal income) and race on black and white graduates' methods of achieving civil rights.

Both whites and blacks supported nonviolent demonstration to the same overwhelming degree (line 13, Table 6.1). Noticeably smaller proportions of whites than blacks supported the other methods. For the most part, personal income, graduate education, years of experience, and employment sector had no significant effect on support of these various methods, and, hence, the relevant data are not shown in Table 6.2. Two exceptions should be mentioned, however. First, support for rent strikes was related significantly with years of experience in five individual samples and all four matched samples (the older a graduate was, the less likely he was to support rent strikes). A difference of 5 years of experience resulted in a decline of from .04 to .10 in the proportion supporting this method. Second, personal income affected black and white graduates' support of work stoppages in different ways. Increasing income was associated with less frequent support from whites but more frequent support from three of the four black samples. In three of the four matched samples, these differences were significant. For blacks, a difference of $5000 corresponded to between 5 and 8 percent willingness to support work stoppages; among whites, to between 3 and 5 percent.

When we controlled for income and the other factors, we found that the effects of race remained uniformly significant for all methods except nonviolent demonstrations. Particularly in their differential support for rent strikes, work stoppages, and busing, the differences between whites and blacks are enormous and important. Most amount to 25 percent or more. Whatever their common education, income, experience, and employment, the two groups of graduates are distinctly different in their views on methods for achieving civil rights.

DISCUSSION

We conclude that a common college degree does *not* homogenize the postcollege characteristics of different racial groups. Black graduates with comparable income, graduate education, years of experience, and employment sector owned their own homes less often (in the MSU group), paid less rent, and owned homes with less property value than did white graduates. As noted, this situation could reflect, among other possibilities, either a choice not to invest as much in housing of comparable quality or a difficulty in finding housing of comparable quality. Black graduates were also less satisfied with their jobs, more often found their most satisfying activity outside their homes and families, and were more active in what they identified as the most important organization to which they belonged.

They also were more likely to contribute money to political causes, to be active in civil rights or other political groups, and to support controversial methods of achieving civil rights. Black graduates more often visited without their wives, and read the Bible more often. In other ways (church attendance, church responsibilities, other kinds of political activities, cultural participation, and visiting practices), black and white graduates were quite similar.

On balance, then, there is clear evidence of both racial differences *and* similarities in graduates' noneconomic characteristics. Relatively speaking, class differences were generally not as influential as racial differences. Higher incomes meant more job satisfaction, more frequent home ownership, more rent, and higher property values, regardless of race; but income differences did not affect most of the other characteristics studied in this chapter. In short, the graduates' common social class characteristics have had a noticeable influence, but racial differences are clearly *not* eliminated by commonality in education, income, years of experience, and/or employment sector.

NOTES

1. These findings conflict with those of other studies, which show that blacks do not participate in organizations as frequently as whites. Furthermore, this dispute is complicated by a debate over the procedure for comparing men with similar socioeconomic status: unlike the studies of Myrdal, Orum, and others, these studies either neglected to control for socioeconomic status (see Campbell, Gurin, and Miller, 1954; Wright and Hyman, 1958) or have explicitly refused to do so (see Hyman and Wright, 1971). However, Hyman and Wright (1971) note that a generally observed increase in voluntary-association memberships has been accompanied by a very sharp increase in black memberships, which is effectively closing the gap between blacks and whites.

2. These variables were chosen largely for their potential to yield useful, interesting information. Certainly, some would be candidates for any formal test of hypotheses formulated from previous work in the area of social participation, but only in these instances does the analysis below approximate such a test.

3. They were similarly asked about the second and third most satisfying activities, but analysis here is confined to the most satisfying activity.

4. This division of familial and extrafamilial activities is not clear-cut for a few individuals. Spouses may share activities of the second type, and individual spouses may join organizations out of concern for their children (school boards, PTAs). Nonetheless the distinction remains generally tenable.

5. Most—86 percent—did; hence we did no further analysis on the simple fact of organizational membership.

6. As with the most satisfying activity, we chose to analyze the level of activity reported for only the most important organization listed. Graduates were assigned scores ranging from 3 ("very active") to 1 ("not active at all").

7. Because of collinearity between graduate education and cumulative grade-point average, and between personal income (here indicating social class) and job status, the latter variable in each pair was excluded from our analysis.

8. Table 6.2 shows the results of this regression for income and, where interesting, for some of the other three variables.

9. The coefficients of these factors are weighted averages of the coefficients of the same factors within each separate matched group. Keeping this fact in mind, we chose to omit these coefficients from Table 6.3. In this chapter, personal income always represents social class.

10. What does the regression coefficient for race mean in such an analysis, compared with the components of regression standardization? If the coefficients from the regression of social participation on personal income, graduate education, years of experience, and employment sector were identical *within* white and black groups, the race coefficient would be identical to the difference of intercepts on the within-group regression lines (that is, the C component). These coefficients are not identical in the general case, so we offer two other interpretations of the race regression coefficient. The first is that it is the vertical distance (scaled in dollars) between the within-group regression lines (or surfaces), measured somewhere between the points on each line that represent the means of all variables in the equation (i.e., approximately the average, vertical distance between the lines). The other interpretation is that this coefficient is the difference in average levels of white and black social participation after controlling for the effects of the other variables in the equation.

11. As we note in Appendix C, the available measures of significance were not strictly appropriate. Futhermore, even if they were appropriate, the dichotomous nature—and, hence, heteroscedasticity—of most dependent variables used would introduce a small margin of uncertainty to the estimation of their significance levels.

12. To arrive at these conventions, we first estimated that it took a $5000 difference in personal income to produce a barely noticeable, reliably observed difference in life style. The impact of race on social participation was measured relative to that estimate. If an increment of under $5000 would produce the same difference in participation as would a racial difference, we decided that income had a greater impact on participation than race. If more than $5000, then race was judged to have the greater relative influence.

Similarly, race and graduate education were considered to have the same impact if the difference between whites and blacks corresponded to the same difference in social-participation level as a difference of 3 years of graduate education. We considered and rejected the use of standardized coefficients at this point because we agree with Cain and Watts (1970) that the weight assigned to the sample standard deviations, in comparison with standardized coefficients, seems unfounded. This point is particularly true in our study: in our data race, scored 1 or 0, had a standard deviation of .5 simply because we used equal numbers of black and white graduates. For a study using a more "representative" population (for example, only 10 percent black), the sample's standard deviation would drop to .3.

13. One might expect a negative correlation of some magnitude between "most satisfying activity" and "type of organization" in which the graduate is most active. We found a modest correspondence between some of the "other" organizations and satisfaction with family activities. Nonetheless, almost all of these correlations (for the various matched groups of graduates) were small (close to zero) and insignificant. Of course, the most satisying activity did not necessarily have to occur within an organization.

14. That is, in every sample where analysis was possible. High multicollinearity and small sample size prohibited computing a regression analysis of the rent paid by MSU whites.

15. We assigned percentages to the response categories as follows: 100 percent white to "mostly white"; 50 percent to "half Negro, half white"; 20 percent to "mostly Negro"; and zero percent to "all Negro."

7

THE FINDINGS:
SUMMARIES,
EXPLANATIONS,
AND IMPLICATIONS_____

> *It is not enough that all individuals start out on even terms, if the members of one group almost invariably end up well to the fore, and those of another far to the rear. . . . As Nathan Glazer has put it, "The demand for economic equality is now not the demand for equal opportunities for the equally qualified; it is now the demand for equality of economic results. . . ."*

DANIEL PATRICK MOYNIHAN (in Rainwater and Yancey, 1967:49)

This study was done on matched samples of black and white college graduates from the same school and year of graduation; each black-white pair had comparable grade-point averages and family social status. In the past, black men have tended to enter, say, education or the ministry in heavier proportions than whites and may, therefore, take education or theological degrees in greater proportions than do white graduates. To minimize the effects of black-white differences in the later choice of a job, we matched white and black classmates so that both groups showed the same distribution of graduates by degree type for each graduation year. The sample included more than 800 black and white male college graduates from two integrated universities (ASU and MSU) and one predominantly Negro university (Frazier) located on the East Coast. The sample members were graduated between 1932 and 1964 (the bulk between 1946 and 1964).

Our data permit some assessment of the effect of equal starting points on success in the marketplace. The possibilities for broad generalization are obviously limited by the small number of universities whose alumni were sampled; furthermore, the blacks from the predominantly Negro university are not classmates of their matching whites. However, the sample members were graduated in the same years, and their schools (by one measure of quality) are quite comparable. We have willingly exchanged generalizability for the quasi-experimental comparability achieved by matched sampling. The findings and implications from Chapters 5 and 6 were discussed at the ends of those chapters and are therefore not restated here. The implications from Chapters 3 and 4, which have not been discussed in this way, are summarized in this chapter, and their possible explanations and implications are discussed.

AVERAGE INCOME-PRODUCING RESOURCES

SUMMARY

We first review the averages and proportions found with regard to graduate education, job status, and personal income. We noted that, on the average, both black graduates *and* their parents have obtained more education than whites, yet work in occupations with less or merely equal status. Thus, while black and white graduates had *similar* grade averages and family social statuses as measured by the status of father's or head of household's job, the fathers and mothers of black graduates averaged 1 to 2 years *more* of education than parents of white graduates, and the black mothers, when employed, held jobs of *lower average status* than those of white mothers. In addition, a higher proportion of black than of white graduates held post-B.A. degrees; thus their average years of schooling leading to such degrees is slightly higher than the whites' average. Yet the average status of current jobs was identical for both groups.

The data on annual incomes—average and median, personal and family—tell different kinds of stories. Median incomes are lower than average incomes by two to three thousand dollars. Because medians reflect the income level at the fiftieth percentile of a sample's income distribution, they indicate more typical, "average" incomes than do genuine averages. Averages are more sensitive to high values—here, the high incomes of relatively few individuals—yet even a few individuals earning more than $16,000 a year (9 percent of all graduates) constitute a result worth considering. Differences in medians favored the white graduates by roughly $1500 in comparisons between black and Frazier graduates, and by roughly $500 in comparisons between black and white classmates. The differences in averages, also favoring whites, were usually greater than the differences in medians. Black graduates compared with MSU whites averaged $1100 less; blacks compared with ASU white graduates earned $1700 to $2300 less. The larger average differences represented the greater, if relatively small, number of white (in contrast to black) graduates with high incomes.

These findings are prima facie evidence that, on the average, blacks are overqualified with respect to their jobs and incomes if, as many assume, education is the prime qualification for jobs and, hence, income. Such overqualification reflects some mixture of discrimination against blacks and self-disqualification by blacks in response to previous and current discrimination. To provide more substantial evidence of discrimination, we analyzed the relations between income and such income-producing resources as education and years of experience in the labor force. This analysis required us first to examine the graduates' backgrounds and job characteristics.

Of the black graduates, most were born in the North (only one group—MSU—has as many as 29 percent southern-born). Their families averaged three siblings (whites' averaged only two). More than half of the blacks came from intact families (a figure still 10 to 20 percent under the 85 percent figure for whites), and their fathers were largely U.S.- and southern-born. In short, these graduates were the "first-generation" sons of black fathers who had "immigrated" to the North. Many of the white graduates were traditional first-generation sons: U.S.-born themselves, about half of their fathers were born abroad. Not surprisingly, the white graduates' religious preferences were divided evenly among the three major religious groups; as was expected, the black graduates were largely Protestant. The whites were urban-born almost as frequently as the blacks and, at the time of our study, resided in suburbs and small towns in considerably larger proportions than the blacks. From 74 to 92 percent of all graduates contacted lived in the New York-New Jersey-Philadelphia region, though we made considerable effort to reach graduates outside this region. Around 20 percent of the Frazier graduates interviewed even lived beyond the adjoining southern and New England regions.

Two occupational characteristics—specific job and employment sector—produced unexpectedly sharp contrasts between the two white graduate samples, and a modest contrast among the black samples. First, over 60 percent of the white ASU graduates were business and other white-collar employees (38 percent) and engineers (25 percent); only 9 percent were secondary school or college teachers. In contrast, MSU white graduates were most frequently teachers (36 percent), and then white collar and business employees (30 percent); only 11 percent were engineers.

The black samples showed modest contrasts. Like their white classmates, a large percentage of MSU black graduates (41 percent) were teachers; the remainder were scattered among many occupations (the largest: business employees—12 percent). ASU blacks were divided primarily into business employees (20 percent) and engineers (18 percent)—to this extent resembling their white classmates. The next largest groups were teachers (16 percent) and social workers (11 percent). Frazier blacks showed a very different pattern. Those compared with ASU whites were most often social workers (26 percent) and teachers (23 percent), while those compared with MSU whites chose fairly evenly among teaching (20 percent), social work (19 percent), medical practice (18 percent), and business (15 percent). Given black graduates' traditional preferences for teaching and the ministry (Johnson, 1938:121-124), we had expected the proportions of black graduates in public-sector jobs to be higher than the proportions of whites, and indeed, overall, 70 percent of three black groups held public-sector jobs, while only 27 percent of ASU whites did so. However, a lesser proportion (roughly 60 percent) of the white MSU graduates and of the fourth black group worked in the public sector.

EXPLANATIONS AND IMPLICATIONS

We noted in Chapter 1 that our primary concern was to determine whether black and white college graduates entering the job market with equal resources were subsequently able to obtain equal job status and personal income. Our finding of virtually equal job status is significant, given Blau and Duncan's (1967) discovery that white men with at least 1 year of college held jobs 16 status units higher than black men. Our rather different finding probably resulted from the effects of at least four factors: regional homogeneity of residence and work locations; greater similarity of backgrounds than is typical for all men (caused by our matched sampling); similarity of undergraduate education; and the (probably) more homogeneous range of jobs available to graduates than to men with some college work short of a degree. Our best guess is that the last factor, reflected in the marked similarity of job distribution in our data (versus the distribution for men with college work short of a degree; see Hare, 1965; Siegel, 1965), is the most important, and that the remaining factors narrow the modest gap remaining to zero. Thus, in our moderately controlled comparison, an equal starting point was converted into one form of equal results—equal average job status.

However, these equalities did not produce equal incomes, either median or average. The median income differences of roughly $500 favoring whites and, to a lesser extent, the $1500 difference (favoring whites) between white and Frazier black graduates are smaller than figures from previous (though not exactly comparable) analyses using 1960 Census data: The smallest of those differences is roughly $3000 (stated in 1959 dollars; also favoring whites). The mean differences—$1100 to $2300—are also noticeably less than those found by previous analysts, whose figures start at $3200 (Siegel, 1965). Of course, the basic reason for these differences is the artificial but illuminating comparability of our graduates. Whites and blacks were deliberately matched according to father's average job status, their own years of experience, and so on. Moreover, graduates clustered moderately into a few specific job categories, many of them (not including business) homogeneous (teachers, doctors, social workers, and engineers, for example). Our sample also showed less variation in regional location of work than would a national sample, and black and white college graduates' income differences were probably less in the North and Northeast than differences aggregated across the United States. Finally, differences in average incomes between black and white graduates of similar schools, whose quality is higher than that of either the average predominantly white or (especially) predominantly black school, *should* be smaller than those found generally.

A more extensive, national study of college graduates is needed to assign relative responsibility to each of these factors. Furthermore, it would be interesting to make similar comparisons of black and white male classmates who terminated their education at various levels prior to receipt of a college degree. If Wohlstetter and Coleman (1970:101) are right that "inadequate standardization involved in equating years of schooling or broad job categories become even less adequate as schooling and higher skill levels increase," we may find the income gap proportionately less for the more educated than has been previously thought.[1]

Apart from these observations, can equalitarians take any comfort from the various median and mean income differences among our graduates, particularly those between graduates with bachelor's degrees only versus postgraduate degrees, and graduates with private- versus public-sector jobs? In our judgment these differences remain important, especially given the unusual comparability of the graduates, the equality of their average job statuses, and the blacks' greater amount of education. The greater spread of white graduates' incomes (in comparison with blacks') above the median, producing the larger mean (in contrast to median) difference, is another and distinctive form of unequal results.

In addition to the four factors noted above, several others might cause these differences. For all men, investment in on-the-job training exceeds the investment in formal schooling. But there may be significant differences in the amount that employers of white (versus black) graduates invest in on-the-job training: for college-educated nonwhites, investment in such training is distinctly less than the investment in formal schooling (Mincer, 1962). There may also be inequalities in our graduates' graduate and professional education. Sample members were graduated from the same or similar undergraduate schools, but subsequently attended different graduate and professional schools. However, this explanation is less persuasive when we note that for the comparisons involving MSU graduates, median and mean income differences are greater for those with bachelor's degrees only than for those with postgraduate degrees. Moreover, sample members in another comparison show comparable differences at all educational levels. (Presumably, any residual inequality of education prior to college entry and graduation has been eliminated by common matriculation, graduation, and similar grade averages.)

Other possibilities are unequal instillation of job-relevant skills (whatever these may be) in college, unequal entry into better-paying jobs (especially in the private sector), unequal training on the job, and unequal subsequent movement into higher-income positions. We cannot assign relative responsibility to these possible factors until we know more about the link between education and work, and about the rewards and skills obtained through formal education and informal training in different parts of the occupational structure.

INCOME-PRODUCING RESOURCES:
ABSOLUTE AND RELATIVE EFFECTS

SUMMARY

Absolute Effects. We examined in detail four important income-producing resources: years of graduate education (leading to a degree), job status, employment sector, and years of experience. In comparison with these four, such factors as grades, family background (e.g., father's education and job status), father's birth location (abroad or in the South), religion (Catholic or non-Catholic), intact or nonintact families, and number of siblings were relatively unimportant. Because the relationships between annual income and the first four resources were little altered by the simultaneous consideration of other possible resources, the bulk of our income analysis focused on the first four. The exceptions are discussed in Chapter 4.

On the average, each additional year of *graduate education* corresponded to about $230 to $970 in annual personal income, with black graduates doing better than whites in three out of four comparisons. Most of these figures approximate or are higher than similar estimates by other researchers (Duncan, 1969; Hauser et al., 1973), though their estimates are largely for additional years of primary, secondary, and undergraduate college rather than postgraduate education. When we controlled for various other income-producing resources not controlled by prior researchers, we found our figures more often larger than, and not merely comparable to, previous estimates. We concluded that these graduates, and perhaps most college graduates generally, were benefiting more from their education than were white and black men generally. The black graduates probably benefited most, since previous researchers had consistently showed the income value of additional education to be less for black men than for white.

Units of *job status* are not as easily interpreted as years of graduate education. However, differences of 10 units generally correspond to meaningful but modest differences in status; note, for example, the rough rank order implicit in the following list of jobs and status units: bank tellers (52), technicians (not elsewhere classified) (62), teachers (72), pharmacists (82), and physicians (92). Ten-unit differences corresponded to income differences of from $400 to $1500. ASU whites did better in this respect than ASU or Frazier–1 blacks, but MSU whites did worse than MSU or Frazier–2 blacks. For black and white males from all educational levels (Duncan, 1969), the same difference in status units meant income differences of $200 for blacks and $700 for whites. When we controlled for differences in the other income-producing resources analyzed by Duncan and by us, black graduates showed greater income differences as a result of job-status differences than did black men generally. Similarly, ASU white graduates surpassed, while MSU whites were essentially comparable to, white men generally.

Additional years of experience usually brought more additional income for white than for black graduates. Four years corresponded to between $1200 and $2000 for white graduates, $800 for three groups of black graduates, and $1600 for a fourth. *Private-* rather than *public-sector employment* also brought more income to whites generally; the differences were $3600 for whites, and $900 and $3000 for blacks.

Relative Effects. Prior research (Duncan, 1969) suggested that education primarily helped white males from all educational levels to obtain jobs with status and, hence, income appropriate to those levels; that is, education's greatest effect on income was indirect. For black males generally, education was shown to have a far greater direct effect on income, despite the fact that white males were absolutely more successful than blacks in translating both education and job status into income. In contrast our analysis showed that *all* groups of graduates used their graduate education more to achieve an income appropriate to their educational level than to obtain a job with a certain status (and, hence, an appropriate income), though both processes occurred.

For black men generally, income directly depended somewhat more on education than on job status; for whites generally, income was determined far more by job status than by education (Duncan, 1969). Our data showed no consistent pattern. MSU black graduates resembled white men generally. White graduates' income depended a bit more on job status than on graduate education, but so did the incomes of two black groups. The greater dependence of income on education found for black males generally was found for only one group of black graduates (Frazier–1).

EXPLANATIONS AND IMPLICATIONS

The explanations and implications of absolute effects are most apparent with regard to the various decompositions performed. We therefore discuss absolute effects after summarizing the findings from the decompositions. This section, then, discusses only the relative effects.

We have noted that education can affect income directly and indirectly (given that we control job status and other variables[2]). If we control job status and say that education directly affects income, we mean that men holding jobs of comparable status have incomes that vary with their education. (Similarly, if we control education and say that job status directly affects income, we mean that men with similar levels of education have incomes that vary with their jobs' statuses.) In contrast, education can have an *indirect* effect on income to the degree that jobs with different status levels require corresponding differences in education but pay their incumbents only according to their status level.

From a simplistic viewpoint, having a direct effect from education that is greater than its indirect effect through job status is unexpected and surprising for four reasons. First, we expect jobs with similar status to require the same minimum level of education (hence the educational levels of men holding such jobs would vary little, over and above that minimum). Second, incomes would then depend primarily on a job's status, even though some variation would result from other factors, such as ability, performance on the job, and hours worked. Third, education's primary effect on income should occur *only* through the access to appropriate jobs that education can provide. Fourth, education should have no direct effect on income because there is no significant variation in levels of education above the minimum required for jobs of similar status.[3] In short, education should have less direct effect than job status on incomes, and its indirect effect through job status should exceed its direct effect.

This view is not consistently supported by analyses of data on either black and white (nonfarm) men generally or our college graduates. If we simply compare the relative, direct determination of income by job status and education, the view is partly supported. Job status is much the stronger determinant for all white men (.3 versus .09) (Duncan, 1969); a more modest but still stronger determinant for white ASU graduates and black MSU graduates; and an even smaller but still greater determinant for MSU whites, ASU blacks, and Frazier–2 graduates. However, if we neglect employment sector and years of experience, then education is much the stronger determinant for both Frazier groups. Moreover, when we compare the direct and indirect effects of education on income, the simplistic view is almost consistently denied by the data for all black men and all of our groups of college graduates.

We can examine some possible explanations for this lack of support. For example, various statistical considerations suggest that for whites generally, the absolute effect of education on job status, and of job status on income, is markedly greater. For both blacks and whites, the absolute effect of education on income is about the same, but incomes and job statuses differ more among whites than among blacks.[4] The result is that white men's individual statuses and incomes are relatively more affected by education and status respectively, but black men's incomes are relatively more determined directly by education.[5]

These differences in income variations probably reflect differences in the average levels of income and status for men generally. Both averages are distinctly lower for blacks than for whites, and thus blacks naturally experience less variation in both. Asking why blacks' average status and income are lower opens a veritable Pandora's box of social and economic issues that range from tax, wage, and welfare policies to the continued impact of racial prejudice in the marketplace. Attempting to explain the greater absolute effect for whites of education and job status is almost as unsatisfactory. We could say that blacks' jobs are less frequently tied to educational requirements. Or, most blacks' job settings are such that their incomes are less affected by job status. Exploring these possibilities requires reconsidering issues related to the different distributions of black and white men across jobs of different sorts. These issues, in turn, point to our ignorance of the uses made by various jobs of different social and mental skills and of the degrees received from various educational institutions. In short, in what ways do such rewards as income depend on education-related qualities over and above those minimally required for each job?

The contrast between findings for black and white men generally and those for our college graduates are thus only partly understandable. Applied to our data, the same statistical considerations just noted lead to a quite different substantive picture.[6] The absolute effect of education on incomes is much greater for our college graduates than for black and white men generally, and slightly greater for black than for white graduates in three out of four comparisons. However, the absolute effect of graduate education on the job status is less for our graduates than for black and white men in general. The absolute effect of job status on income was greater for our graduates than for black and white men generally, and differences among graduates' incomes were much greater than for blacks and whites generally. The net result of these findings is that from level of education, we can estimate a college graduate's income better than we can the income of white or black men generally; however, knowing job status gives us no more help in estimating incomes for graduates than for whites or blacks generally.

As before, seeking explanations for these results leads us to consider the different job distributions for white and black graduates in contrast to white and black men generally. Consider briefly some characteristics of the specific occupations that our graduates held. For example, teachers' salaries (and, hence, much of their incomes) are determined by their degrees, additional education credits (which sometimes lead to advanced degrees), and years of experience. Thus education can easily affect teachers' incomes over and above the minimal educational requirements for specific jobs. Social workers' incomes may behave similarly, although this job category is here defined broadly enough to encompass the administrative positions above the caseworker level that are normally held by those with postgraduate degrees. Public-sector employees' incomes may also be more closely determined by level of education than are those of private-sector employees. If so, the larger direct (versus indirect) effect of education on income for blacks particularly—since they hold public-sector employment more frequently than whites—but also for most of our graduates, makes sense.

However, this hypothesis seems inapplicable to engineers, doctors, or business employees. Whether within or outside of academe, engineers' and doctors' incomes should be relatively insensitive to additional education beyond that required to qualify for the job initially. Likewise, business employees' educational credentials should have little effect on their incomes, once a specific job status has been acquired. Modest variations in level of education are all we should expect among those holding jobs of similar status. Again, then, we are left with our inadequate knowledge of the relationship between education, on-the-job training, income, and job status for different occupations and for groups of black and white men.[7]

DECOMPOSING PERSONAL-INCOME DIFFERENCES

SUMMARY

The Entire Sample. Following our analysis of absolute and relative effects on income, we decomposed the average income differences between black and white graduates into the *A component*, due to differences in the average level of each of the four major income-producing resources; the *B component*, due to differences in the absolute effect of each resource on income; and the *C component*, reflecting average income differences among men with the minimum amount of each resource (such as a B.A. degree only, or little work experience subsequent to college graduation). The *C component* also served as an index of the effects of all possible income-producing resources other than the four major ones.

Decomposition permits a distinction between merely increasing individual resources and changing either the income value or the general effect on income of given resources. Prior policies and popular assumptions have ignored the latter two components and presumed that something akin to the former, particularly differences in average educational levels, was the cause of racial inequality. This situation is understandable: Politically and for policy making, it is easier to increment the *average level* of whatever individual resources produce income than to tamper with the income *value* of those resources. Here we summarize our general findings and those from our subgroup analyses.

The ASU Group. In general, our findings were structurally similar to those of prior studies of white and black males at all educational levels. The picture is one of diverging incomes with increasing income-producing resources, and conversely, of converging incomes among men with lesser amounts of such resources. The largest, and positive, part of the average income difference proved to be the *B component.*[8] Thus white graduates' greater average income resulted from their greater degree of success in converting job status and years of experience into income, compared to blacks. These two variables were associated with average income differences ranging from $1900 to $2700 (job status) and $2550 to $2700 (years of experience), figures larger than or comparable to the ASU group's overall average income differences of $1795 and $2370.

The *B component* was partly offset by the *C component*, whose large negative value indicated that black graduates in the middle-to-low range of resources were doing as well as or better than whites with comparably modest resources. The *A component*, here favoring whites, constitutes the remaining difference in average incomes—roughly half of the overall difference. Consistent with our reanalysis of previous findings for national samples by Coleman et al. (1972) and by Blum (1972) and Duncan (1969), this component is usually the smallest of the three in terms of percentages, though it is still important. Our data showed that the higher proportion of white than black graduates holding private- versus public-sector jobs was primarily responsible for the size of the *A component*. These higher proportions provided whites with about $1000 worth of the overall difference.

The MSU Group.   The comparisons involving MSU whites produced different results from the above. As we have learned, MSU whites were quite different from ASU whites. They held public-sector employment in almost equal proportions as their black counterparts, and 36 percent were teachers. The Frazier graduates were also unusual: of all groups, theirs included the highest percentage of M.D.'s (18 percent). These specific differences naturally affected our results. More broadly, we were decomposing noticeably smaller mean differences: $1000, rather than $1700 to $2300. We first found that differences in the average level of income-producing resources were either negligible or negative (that is, relative to the ASU comparison, black graduates averaged more such resources). On the average, *all* groups of black graduates completed more graduate education than did whites, but in only one of the MSU comparisons (MSU whites and Frazier–2 graduates) did this advantage amount to a relatively large income difference ($500).

Second, both the MSU and the Frazier–1 black graduates had more advantages over MSU whites when converting some of their resources into income. Thus, the blacks' incomes approached the whites' in higher-status jobs. The white graduates retained the overall *B component* advantage when compared with black MSU classmates, because the former still derived more income from additional experience (as above) and private-sector employment. However they relinquished this advantage when compared with Frazier–2 graduates, largely because of a considerable income convergence among those with high-status jobs (most of which were held by the M.D.'s mentioned above). Added experience also paid more to Frazier–2 blacks than to MSU whites, though MSU whites received more additional income from private-sector employment.

Employment Sector and Degree Levels. Finally, we wanted to determine whether the overall decompositions held also for four major subgroups of graduates: those holding bachelor's degrees only versus postgraduate degrees, and those with public- versus private-sector employment. Given the larger proportions of white graduates employed in the private sector, and of black graduates holding postgraduate degrees, these two variables could actually affect income in a different manner than was reflected in the overall figures and could help explain the different pictures obtained from the ASU and the MSU group comparisons. The subgroup findings largely supported those from the decomposition of ASU-group income differences: white incomes diverge from black incomes as income-producing resources increase.

However, the MSU-group comparisons revealed some complexities. For those with bachelor's degrees only and private-sector employment, whites' incomes diverged from blacks' as resources increased. Both the median and the mean income differences were consistently and substantially greater for these graduates than for those with postgraduate degrees and those holding public-sector jobs. For the latter, black graduates' incomes *converged* with whites' as job status and years of experience increased; in addition, the mean and median black and white income differences were usually either positive but small (thus favoring whites) or negative (favoring blacks; for example, Frazier–2 graduates with postgraduate degrees reported higher median and mean incomes than whites).

In short, we uncovered similar patterns for postgraduate degree holders and public-sector employees on the one hand, and for bachelor's degree holders and private-sector employees, on the other. Only the patterns for the latter two groups are completely consistent across both the ASU- and the MSU-group comparisons. Both the subgroup and the overall findings indicate that the income value of various income-producing resources varies with and depends on rather different distributions of graduates to specific occupational groups, advanced degrees, and employment sectors.

EXPLANATIONS AND IMPLICATIONS

Any adequate explanation of these results must confront some of the same issues already discussed. In particular, what explains black-white differences in the absolute effects on income of each factor? The answers at hand are no more satisfactory than were our earlier suggestions. A sound descriptive explanation of such findings requires expanding our present knowledge of the uses made by various occupations of educational qualifications, years of experience, and so forth. Why is it that whites and blacks with equal resources are paid different amounts (whites receive more) regardless of employment sector? Why is it that for the MSU group, added job status closes the income gap for public-sector employees while enlarging it for those in the private sector?

Even with answers to these questions, we would still need to explain observed differences in the distribution of graduates into various job categories. Why, for example, did Frazier graduates eventually become M.D.'s and social workers in such large numbers, compared with MSU and ASU graduates? Answering such questions requires studying such questions as: What career education (if any) is built into a college experience? What influence do peers, parents, and relatives have on graduates' job choices? The answers to these questions, unfortunately, may be particular to specific cohorts of graduates, faculty, and parents, and hence continually changing.

Lacking answers to these questions, we limit discussion here to the implications of our component analyses for the framing of a policy that will produce equal results—equal job status and incomes—for comparably equipped and employed black and white graduates. Assume for the moment that either we understood enough about the links between income, education, experience, and so on to know how to change the various components and thus reduce the income gap, or, adequate understandings aside, someone simply wanted to change the contributions of various components to the income gap (probably common practice in policy making). Assume also that our findings came from a large enough sample to warrant the creation of new, national policies. Or, that these decompositions had been replicated and validated for black and white college graduates in a large metropolitan area, and that some governmental agency or agencies wanted to implement policies that would guarantee equal results in this geographical area. The motive for such action might be either a concern for justice and the reduction of discriminatory practice, or a belief that such results would have economic benefits for that area beyond those accruing to the individual graduates.

Third, assume the continuity of our findings. Drawing policy implications for the future from data that reflect past social conditions (here the absolute effects and average resource levels of 1966–67) presumes continuity, not necessarily of the exact figures but of the magnitude and direction of present findings (that is, the positive or negative percentage of the income gap contributed by each component should not have changed by more than 20 percent of the current—1966–67—gap). We also presume that any potential change in the income values of resources will increase or decrease the incomes of all people, regardless of what resource level they possess.[9]

Fourth, our decompositions and suggested applications to policy assume that if change is needed, the income value of black graduates' resources and the average level of those resources should (ordinarily) be changed so as to approximate the values and levels of whites' resources. This assumption follows whenever black graduates' average resources, and the income values of those resources, are less than those of white graduates, as are those of black men relative to white men generally. It also presumes the desirability, thus far generally reflected in social policy, of increasing blacks' levels and values rather than decreasing those of whites.[10] Finally, we also assume, for similar reasons, that the income value of resources will increase rather than decrease, in the event that they change or are changed through the implementation of policy. Nevertheless, policy makers should consider techniques for desensitizing incomes to the differential possession of certain resources *if* those resources prove to be less relevant than Americans generally believe to either job performance or the distribution of qualified people into various jobs.

The Overall Picture. Equal results show up in the component analysis of an income gap when there are no income-value differences for given amounts of education, experience (that is, no *B component*), and no average-income differences between blacks and whites with similar amounts of education, experience, and so forth (that is, no *C component*). However, in the short run, and for all practical purposes, any gap, even in average incomes (the *A component*), constitutes unequal results.[11] Our findings clearly suggest the need to achieve equal average incomes, but they do not prescribe any *one* way to achieve that goal: for all but one comparison, we observed diverging incomes with increasing resources; for the fourth, converging incomes.

For the more typical case of diverging incomes, our decomposition indicates that a policy that first raised the average level of black graduates' resources to that of the average level of white graduates' resources would eliminate only half of the income gap, if that much (see, for example, the case of MSU whites and blacks). This goal could be achieved simply by increasing the proportion of black graduates in the private sector by some 30 to 40 percent. However, as long as the slopes and income levels diverge as resources increase, raising black graduates' average resources will not be as effective in the first three comparisons as in the fourth, where incomes converge. In addition, given the divergence of incomes and the relative size of each component, we would probably have to increase the income values for black graduates of higher-status jobs and of greater experience to the levels that hold for white graduates. Furthermore, to achieve equal results for MSU whites and blacks, we would have to increase the income value for blacks of private-sector employment to its present value for whites.

In the comparison involving converging incomes, black graduates have an advantage (in contrast to the blacks involved in the three other comparisons) with respect to their greater level of average resources. In this case the basic source of income inequality is the greater income value of job status and of years of experience for white than for black graduates with below-average (below 74) job status and few to moderate (2 to 8) years of experience. For both diverging and converging incomes, then, the more effective technique is to change the income values of the resources. This technique would be more fundamental than merely increasing the average level of a group's resources. In addition, such policies would be more difficult to conceptualize and implement: They would require more political decisions than would policies designed simply to increment the average levels of a given group's resources. Moreover, whether intentional or not, such decisions have rarely been made other than as parts of tax and wage policies, although increasing resource levels has often been the focus of policies and programs such as Headstart and Job Corps.

Note, however, that these analyses can suggest different and alternative approaches to attaining equal results. Reducing the largest positive component is only one strategy. For example, in the case of converging incomes (among MSU whites and Frazier-2 blacks), we suggest the possibility of further increasing the present black advantage at various points. One would thus raise the income values for blacks of both high-status jobs and many years' experience to the point that such values further exceeded those for whites. The result, if carried far enough, would be no *net* income gap. Thereafter, one could work toward comparability of income values across all levels of all resources. The eventual result would be equal results as represented by the presence of negligible *B* and *C components,* and (probably) negligible *A components.*

In short, we suggest first attempting to reduce large, positive components (and subcomponents for individual resources). However, large components, whether positive or negative, do not necessarily mean that a policy designed to reduce that size at a later date will be easier or less costly to implement. Our figures do not indicate what approach would be easiest; strictly speaking, they only show where the bulk of a recent (or present) income gap is to be found given the assumptions we made earlier. We recommend attacking the large components first, if possible. Alternative policies focused on other subcomponents may, however, be easier to pursue, or may at least be more justifiably pursued in the search for equal results—equal average personal incomes.[12]

The Subgroup Pictures. The subgroup decompositions suggested additional policy recommendations. Given our findings and the concentration of our graduates in the New York, New Jersey, and Philadelphia regions, *any* general recommendation should be qualified to allow for modest to major variations by region and by employment sector. Thus, for example, the income gap between MSU white and black graduates is largest for private-sector employees, and any attempt to change the income value of job statuses for MSU blacks must consider the different contribution of job status to income by employment sector. In the private sector, the income value of black graduates' higher-status jobs must be raised; in the public sector, those of low-to-middle-status jobs need raising. Moreover, the private-sector gap is much greater. Therefore, raising the former will contribute more to the goal of overall, equal results than will raising the latter, though both courses of action should be pursued. Unfortunately, changing the income value of either experience or job status is probably far more possible in the public than the private sector.

There is a methodological lesson in this discussion for policy making based on research findings. The numbers may give wise counsel to contrasting policies and suggest likely sources of difficulty that ought not be ignored; however, they will not usually imply an optimal or sole possible policy. The link between the implications of findings and subsequent policy making is precarious and in need of research as a separate topic.

The Self-Fulfilling Prophecy. Our data also suggest the probable invalidity of a long-standing, widely held belief that simply increasing the qualifications (especially the educational level) of individual blacks would ameliorate racial discrimination. The young W.E.B. DuBois subscribed to his mother's teaching that

> The secret of life and the loosing of the color bar, then, lay in excellence, in accomplishment; if others of my family, of my color kin, had stayed in school, instead of quitting early for small jobs, they could have risen to equal whites. . . . There was not real discrimination on account of color—it was all a matter of ability and hard work. (Logan, 1944:33)

His "program of life," unchanged after his residence as Fisk University, centered on "a group of educated Negroes, who from their knowledge and experience would lead the mass" (Logan, 1944:38). St. Clair Drake (1962) expressed similar ideas. This deep faith in education has a long history; it was cited as an underlying premise for the founding of Negro colleges in much earlier days (Johnson, 1938:276), and a current version of it emphasizes remedial or compensatory education for black children.

Familiar, too, are exhortations by blacks and whites alike that blacks "do better with what they already have" (Sutherland, 1942:100), and not disqualify themselves in the face of expected discrimination. Decrying the lack of enrollment of blacks in a vocational training course, a 1941 NAACP Bulletin commented:

> There can be no justifiable basis for hue and cry about discrimination against our workers unless there are available men qualified to step into jobs when they are open. The reluctance of many men to spend time training for jobs in industries which bar them because of color is understandable, but so shortsighted an attitude will be fatal to the well-being of the race if allowed to persist. (Sutherland, 1942:101)

Those who believe that increasing the qualifications of individual blacks will significantly reduce the present degree of economic inequality assume that skin color is only one more characteristic of social class. More precisely, the disadvantages of skin color are little more than the disadvantages of social-class background and class-related abilities. The lower-class stereotype of blacks that some hold—what Degler (1969) called a "class interpretation of racial prejudice"—is an expression of this assumption. Viewed from the perspective of this book, policies that try to solve the problem of discrimination against blacks by increasing individual abilities are actually trying to increase the average level of blacks' income-producing resources—that is, decrease the negative effect of the A component. The question, then, is: How is increasing the level of blacks' resources, especially the quantity and quality of their schooling, to reduce discrimination? The answer may seem obvious, but close examination shows that the theory generally propounded as an answer is debatable.

The theory is that a self-fulfilling prophecy in reverse can reduce both the discriminatory tendencies of the white majority and the self-disqualification of the blacks. Traditionally, the prophecy has moved from the belief in black inferiority to the reality of educational and economic inequality, and back to reinforcement of the belief without any certain starting point. In reverse, the movement is from actual, partial reduction of at least some types of inequality to belief in the irrelevance of color in the marketplace, and back to a fuller, snowballing realization that full economic equality is achievable.

One possible source of the initial, partial reduction of inequality is governmental and philanthropic programs designed to upgrade the schooling and other resources of individual blacks. Another possible starting point, one not entailing governmental action, is the alleged impact of clearly visible, exceptional black men distinguished by outstanding occupational and educational achievements. Their existence presumably testifies to an apparent reduction in inequality. In theory, their example induces more positive beliefs about blacks' abilities among whites and blacks alike, which in turn leads to further reductions in inequality. This "doctrine of exceptionalism" has often been expressed by noted black intellectuals. DuBois, writing at the turn of the century, believed that "the Talented Tenth of the Negro race must be made leaders of thought and missionaries of culture among their people. . . . The Negro race, like all other races, is going to be saved by its exceptional man" (Fishel and Quarles, 1967:369). More recently, Sir Arthur Lewis wrote that "the measure of whether we are winning our battle is in how many of us rise to the middle and [particularly, in the context of our research] the top" (1969:9). "The road to the top in the great American corporations and other institutions is through higher education" (1969:10).

Unfortunately, this emphasis on the exceptional achievements of blacks and their possible effect on future inequality (see also Alsop, 1967:23) reflects some naiveté about the operation of self-selection in discriminatory contexts. By focusing on the need to change the average level of blacks' income-producing resources (hence reduce the A component), this perspective implicitly accepts the fact that blacks' resources currently have less income value than whites' (that is, it maintains the B component). In short, this thinking sanctions continued discrimination. For our research, the empirical question was whether reducing a positive A component (noting exceptional blacks and even expanding their numbers) would actually mitigate discrimination as effectively as reducing, say, a positive B component.

Let us presume, for some reason, that the proportion of exceptional, or at least well-qualified, blacks increases. Black awareness of this increase might reduce self-disqualification and, hence, the impact of the remaining white discrimination; and whites' awareness of this increase might reduce their discriminatory practices. Or, it might decrease self-disqualification by blacks with above-average or exceptional qualifications (because they are part of the upgrading process), but increase self-disqualification by blacks with below-average qualifications (because they are left out of this same process). Or, operation of the self-fulfilling prophecy might reduce white discrimination and/or black self-disqualification only after a threshold point has been reached—perhaps, say, 20 percent of all proprietors, managers, and professionals would have to be black (unfortunately, such a threshold might remain beyond blacks' reach as long as discrimination continues at its present level). Or, the highly visible, exceptional blacks might have very little effect on discrimination/self-disqualification. In short, corollaries of the self-fulfilling prophecy theory presume that beneficial effects will trickle down from exceptional blacks to all others, but the presumptions do not necessarily hold.

Certainly the exceptional blacks' achievements should have some beneficial effects. As Sir Arthur Lewis wrote, "If we did conquer the top it would make much easier the conquering of the middle—both in our own minds, and in other people's minds, by altering our young people's image of themselves and of what they can achieve" (1969:10). But would it also alter the feelings and cognitions of whites, particularly those holding other than executive or professional positions? Let us assume that a great many more blacks than at present were perceived to be equally qualified for "good" positions at all job levels above the semiskilled. Before a reduction of discrimination occurred, other, accompanying conditions might be required. For example, Blau and Duncan (1967:224) noted that the gap in the South between the proportions of white and black men completing grammar school began to narrow "only after more than 60 percent of the whites had reached this educational level." Perhaps, they speculated, "the dominant white group relaxes discriminatory practices and permits Negroes in growing numbers to attain a certain level of education only after a clear majority of its own members have already attained this level." Similarly, it may be that the degree to which black men with a given level of education are rewarded with specific jobs and income levels depends on the proportions of whites and/or blacks who have already reached that level. Finally, a very real possibility is that equalizing qualifications might be counterproductive by causing increased black-white competition in at least some job categories, accompanied by a form of racial discrimination devoid of the usual class interpretations. Indeed, this situation may already be occurring in certain skilled occupations.

In short, popular beliefs regarding the self-fulfilling prophecy have very questionable foundations. In addition, support for policies that center exclusively on changing the *A component* are based on a questionable belief in the social rationality and moral acceptability of unequal income values (expressed in the *B component*). Our decompositions redirect attention to equalizing the income values of resources, because the gap in average black and white resources is simply a less important component of the income gap than is the component representing the structural inequality of the value of the resources.

NOTES

1. The importance of standardizing on distributions as well as on means can be further illustrated by our study. Part of the difference in income gaps found by our two sets of comparisons was caused not only by the different white comparison groups, but also by the different distributions (within the ASU and MSU groups) by year of graduation. Graduates in the MSU group were "older" than those in the ASU group. Fewer of the former had been graduated in or near 1964, the last graduation year sampled. This was true even though the mean years of experience for all groups was essentially the same—10 to 11 years. Thus, if we standardize the MSU group's data to the ASU group's years of experience but retain their present incomes per year of graduation, the $1555 average income difference between MSU white and black graduates—$1532—approaches the $1794 difference between ASU whites and blacks fairly closely. However, the MSU white, Frazier-2 black difference is little affected by a similar standardization.

2. In Duncan's analysis: number of siblings, and the education and job status of respondents' fathers or heads of household; here, years of experience and employment sector. Job status excepted, the particular variables controlled generally have not affected the different ways that education produces income and will not be specifically mentioned unless they do.

3. If ability as shown on the job and rewarded in income is the same ability shown by IQ tests, and IQ and education are so correlated that years of education completed represents both schooling and ability; or if on-the-job ability is produced by on-the-job training which, in turn, varies with the possession of educational credentials over and above the minimum required; *then* education *would*, in the present discussion, be judged a factor directly determining income. We discount both possibilities here only for lack of data.

4. This statement is a substantive translation of variance premised on the theorem that the "variance of a variable can be computed as half the mean square of all variate differences" (see Winsborough et al., 1963:978).

5. In contrast to whites' incomes, black men's incomes show a greater direct effect from education than an indirect effect through job status for two reasons. First, while variations in the levels of black and white men's educational levels are nearly equal, there is far less variation in black incomes to explain ($2000 versus $5700 standard deviations), yet additional education brings about the same income increment to blacks and whites ($120 and $160 respectively; based on Duncan, 1969, and using years of education rather than his scale of educational attainment as the independent variable). The partial result is that black men's incomes directly depend more on education than on either job status or education indirectly (through job status). Second, there is also far less variation in job status among black men (standard deviation, 16.9) than among whites (24.6); but for whites, the greater increment of status from added education, and the greater

increment of income from added status, offset this lesser variation. For whites, the result is a greater effect of education on job status, and of job status on income, relative to that of education on income.

6. The following statistics are relevant to subsequent discussion. The standard deviations for the resources of white graduates are: graduate education, 1.54 to 1.59 years; job status, 12.1 to 13.7 units; income, $6270 to $8340. For black graduates the standard deviations are: graduate education, 1.6 to 2.4 years; job status, 12.5 to 13.3 units; income, from $4511 to $7611.

7. Sharp's (1970:51–57, 63–69) discussion of the fit between college learning and careers is relevant to the above discussion.

8. Positive components indicate an advantage to white graduates; negative, an advantage to black graduates.

9. That is, the line showing the income value of a resource would rotate around a point representing those with the fewest resources. This rules out tax policies that would change the income value of some people's resources by either supplementing incomes below, or confiscating them above, a certain level. Furthermore, if for any reason an agency wanted its policy to change the income-value structure first, and *then* change average resource levels (or otherwise change income values in a manner inconsistent with that just described), it should utilize a different component analysis as its basis. For example, it could use a decomposition that first equalized slopes and then averaged resource levels. For further discussion, see Appendix D.

10. We also doubt the political pragmatism of reducing these levels and/or values for either group, although either or both could be considered as ways to achieve racial equality and other goals. For example, given the number of available jobs that require higher education for their adequate performance, the average level of educational attainment and its income value could change in response to the present overproduction of college graduates with advanced degrees. If one desires to reduce either factor for white graduates, the figures from this decomposition do not strictly apply, though it is likely that the same resources (and their subcomponents) would be important in the relevant decomposition. That decomposition would merely exchange the racial groups associated with the weights for the difference of slopes and means used in the present decomposition. See Althauser and Wigler (1972), and Appendix D.

11. The significance of any remaining component due to group differences in average resources depends on whether those differences are associated with unequal opportunities or inequality of another kind. Group differences unassociated with either would cause some part of an income gap that could not be interpreted as evidence of unequal results. Thus unequal average job status for our graduates would constitute unequal results of another kind, as would the unequal proportions of black and white graduates either employed in the private sector or holding graduate degrees. Any difference due to differences in mean years of experience, *as we define experience*, would not constitute an unequal opportunity. Neither would differences in the mean age of black and white men in general. However, if experience is defined as actual years of full-time civilian employment rather than the time elapsed since college graduation, differences in mean experience *would* constitute unequal opportunity.

12. The contrast between our approach to policy and that found in Jencks et al. (1972) and elsewhere is clear. The simple fact that income-producing resource is not presently associated with a substantial portion of an income gap does not mean it could not be profitably changed to effect beneficial social goals. Nor does the small percent of income variation explained by a given resource prohibit the possibility that a policy could (deliberately or accidentally) create social conditions in which that resource explained *more* variance (i.e., becomes "more important"). One possible, initial effect of Jenck's suggested income policy—to reduce variation and, thereby, inequality in incomes—could be to *increase* the percent of variance explained by the factors he considered. Thus a larger amount of a lesser variance would be explained.

8

OTHER IMPLICATIONS, AND DIRECTIONS FOR THE FUTURE_____

It is precisely in regard to their policy impact that the findings and interpretations of social scientists must be subjected to the most rigorous critical analysis. In these areas of social justice and equity the contributions of social scientists can only be accepted as merely one of the many considerations to be taken into account in arriving at policy decisions.

KENNETH CLARK (1973:120)

T wo further matters can be addressed from our analysis. One is the income value of a degree from a predominantly black (in contrast to integrated) college. The other is the directions to be taken in future research.

DEGREE VALUE

Does a degree from a predominantly black school have the same value in the marketplace as a degree from an integrated school? Do both types equally counteract, if necessary, any previous disadvantages with which their recipients began college, instill market-relevant skills in their holders, and certify them as trainable for postcollege jobs, assuming that either or both types of degrees do these things to a significant and measurable degree?

Our observations are necessarily limited. We deliberately drew respondents from only three schools, representing an above-average level of educational quality. Frazier, the predominantly black university included in the study, represents the best of the predominantly black schools. In addition, we did not extensively examine graduates' postcollege and professional training (beyond asking respondents to report the number of years they had attended and the degrees they had received); measure the possibly different skills and resources

141

brought to college or acquired there; nor link these skills and resources to graduates' subsequent jobs. In short, the economic fortunes of our graduates are no basis for conclusions regarding the viability of black colleges and universities in general. Nevertheless, previous findings of similarly limited scope have served as modest antidotes to the controversial findings from such less confined (and presumably more generalizable) studies as Jencks's (1972) and Coleman's (1966; see discussion in Edmonds et al., 1973:89–91).

Given these caveats and our limited concern with equal economic results, we now draw some modest conclusions that are implicit in our four black-white comparisons. On the whole, our data showed that the black graduates from the predominantly black university did almost as well as the blacks from the two integrated schools. Seven findings support this statement.

1. Frazier graduates usually had lower median and mean annual income differences than ASU and MSU black graduates, but the differences were on the order of $500 to $700. One was larger—$1100—and one was zero.
2. In the employment sector and degree comparisons, Frazier graduates did not usually do as well as the other black graduates; income differences were larger than those just cited. However, exceptions were more noticeable. Among those with either postgraduate degrees or private-sector employment, Frazier graduates had greater average or median incomes.
3. Graduate education had consistently greater income value for Frazier graduates than for other black graduates.
4. Frazier graduates' incomes converged with MSU white graduates' incomes as education, job status, and experience increased.
5. Regarding the distributions of graduates to different occupational groups, an unusually large proportion—18 percent—of Frazier graduates become doctors.
6. ASU black graduates' distribution into specific occupations more closely resembled that of typical (ASU) whites than that of any other black group.
7. All the black groups did far better than black men generally (as did the white graduates in comparison with white men generally, though to a lesser extent than blacks) with regard to average income, job status, and income values of additional education and of job status.

Without more knowledge about their causes, these differences are not consistent enough to reflect negatively on the marketplace value of a Frazier degree.

DIRECTIONS FOR FUTURE RESEARCH

Our research and others' previous research exhibits three interrelated weaknesses. First, we lacked the ability to explain our overall findings descriptively and, hence, to construct a specific picture of the disaggregated processes and relationships that our analyses revealed. We also lacked the ability to construct theoretical models that would explain and illuminate our data; we needed models that included both the actual (in contrast to the "supposed") functions of formal schooling and specific degrees for distributing graduates into specific jobs carrying various statuses and incomes. Finally, we felt hampered by our inability to move confidently back and forth between policy making and the kinds of statistics and findings most relevant to policy. The following recommendations might remedy these inadequacies.

DESCRIPTIVE ADEQUACY

To advance the state of the art in this area, we need to focus more attention on (1) the characteristics of the jobs men hold, just as attention is now given to the jobholders' characteristics; (2) the processes by which jobs' characteristics affect and are affected by the distribution of people's job-relevant (and job-irrelevant) resources; and (3) the processes by which people possessing characteristics and resources (actually and supposedly) relevant to a variety of jobs are ultimately distributed into different occupations and different income levels.

Our recommendations are prompted, in part, by the sometimes unexplained, but nevertheless striking, differences in the distributions of black and white classmates into different specific jobs. Probing the origins of these differences *could* lead us toward a more intensive, longitudinal study of the college experience and of its specific effects on graduates' movement into variously described jobs (Bowman, 1972). More generally, this implies a greater concern for the distribution-dependence of many of our statistics and greater emphasis on the study of distributions[1] relative to the present emphasis on such measures of central tendency as means and medians. We also need to examine the effects of peers, parents, fluctuating job opportunities, and relative prestige across different jobs at such crucial times in adolescent and post-adolescent schooling as when undergraduates declare their majors or sign up for job interviews (see Sharp, 1970). The answers to these questions should point to other, probably economic and certainly theoretical, directions for further research.

We recommend greater emphasis on the study of job characteristics partly because of the rather uneven distribution of graduates into specific occupational groups—the partial clustering of graduates in teaching, medicine, and social work, for example. In attempting to interpret the income values of different resources, we became aware that we were, in effect, averaging the respective income values of each resource across men clustered heterogeneously into different kinds of employment. This situation raised questions (see Kaysen, 1973) about the quality and meaning of such averages, both for this and for broader samples of men and jobs. For example, Wohlstetter and Coleman (1970:64) point out that schooling may be less relevant to maximizing earnings in the occupations most frequently held by blacks, in contrast to those held by whites. The same may be true for different types of occupations: professions versus others; private- versus public-sector employment; unionized versus other employment; and so on. The point is not to discard such averages but to decompose them into their significant components and thereby to enhance our understanding of their meaning.

We took a first step in this direction by considering the relationship between graduates' personal incomes and various resources within four subgroups: bachelor's degree only versus graduate degree holders, and public- versus private-sector employees. A more general investigation into the uses of education, experience, and so forth by similar or even smaller subgroups would require two more steps. First, we would have to disaggregate national samples or local samples like ours into smaller and relatively homogeneous subgroups, defined by combinations of job categories, employment sector, geographic region, and other variables (as was done by Eckaus, 1973, for example). Next, we would study the relationship between income and education, experience, and so forth within these subgroups through statistical analyses and other appropriate methods, possibly including informal interviews with employers and employees about the role of education, experience, and other resources. (A word of caution: the results of such methods might produce more folklore than fact, if Berg's (1970) excursions in this direction are replicated.)

Further steps should include analyses of the actual requirements of different jobs, the relationships between these requirements and educational degrees, performance measures or ratings, entry and promotion criteria, and the processes of self-selection and recruitment that operate for different jobs.[2] We would then reaggregate the uses of each resource with its corresponding income values, according to the respective distributions of each sample's constituents in each subgroup. This procedure would produce a more satisfactory, descriptive explanation of the decomposed difference between group means than resulted from our subgroup analysis.

Eventually, subject to the limitations of the small sample sizes we might have to work with, we might be able to extract a small number of subgroup combinations that were homogeneous with respect to their typical relationships between income and various resources. Such an outcome would mitigate the obvious practical problems in this approach. Large samples would be needed. Even in a national sample, only the most heavily populated job categories would yield large enough subsamples to warrant this sort of study. The hope for some homogeneous use of both resources and their income values, for either single subgroups or subgroup combinations that could be adequately sampled, would be precarious, and the larger the subgroup, the more precarious our hope would become. Subdividing some job categories, for example, salaried business employees into those employed by "small" versus "large," or local versus interstate and/or international firms, might also be warranted and would create additional sampling problems.

The only alternative approach appears to be the use of less detailed, descriptive explanations of aggregated data together with reliance on the development of theoretical explanations applicable to aggregates, however heterogenous the mix of uses and income values of resources actually involved in the aggregates.

THEORETICAL ADEQUACY

Several factors indicate the need for theoretical models that enable us to make sense of statistical results. One is that we could learn more by even roughly comparing theoretical expectations with empirical findings than by doing only detailed, descriptive investigations, even though the latter are of much value to the former. Consider our attempts to understand differences between black and white graduates, and between black and white men in general. Why were there differences in the absolute and relative effects of income-producing resources? Job status, as measured by Duncan's socioeconomic index, has been central to many empirical studies of social stratification in the last 10 years. If we recall the derivation of Duncan's index, we may gain some perspective on group differences involving job status.

This index, based on the educational and income characteristics of occupational groups, merges both characteristics into a single value. If we think of it, imprecisely, as indicating the averge income and education of men in a given job category, then the effect of job status on individual graduates' incomes becomes the degree to which the education and income, or socioeconomic status, typical of all persons in that category determines an individual's income. The effect of an individual's educational level on his personal income then becomes the degree to which income depends on education *over and above* the effect of the education/income typical of all persons in that category. In short, the high or low incomes of individuals with varying amounts of education may represent much more or much less income than this sort of job typically brings. The question then becomes: According to various models, how much income variation due to individual educational levels can we expect, relative to that resulting from the education/income typical of all men in similar job categories?

At minimum, the black-white differences that we observed strongly suggest that the graduates' incomes were differently distributed relative to jobs and educational levels, and by different processes. One attempt to speculate on similar findings was offered by Coleman et al. (1972:294), who found that "income is the more important dimension of occupational achievement for blacks, toward which their education and other background resources are utilized, while occupational status is the more important dimension for whites." This and prior analyses led these authors to a voluntaristic interpretation of their findings: Whites and blacks adopt different long-range career strategies. Whites try to use their education and other resources to obtain high-status, low-income initial jobs; they then attempt to convert these resources into later jobs with high incomes. Blacks, in contrast, tend more to employ their resources to obtain early jobs with high incomes; they later try, with less success, to maintain the income levels of their early jobs in their later jobs.

This interpretation seems to impute intentional career strategies, cultural preferences, or other forms of rational and nonrational choice to blacks and whites in order to explain differences in the relationships among education, job status, and income for whites and blacks. It is possible, of course, that these differences in preference and strategy merely reflect underlying social structural or market mechanisms. The important point is simply that we need both theoretical models that explain the origins of these preferences and their relationships to various mechanisms, and additional empirical evidence supporting one or another model.

We frequently found ourselves well short of understanding, either from this or earlier research, the complete mutual effects of formal schooling, job status, experience, income, and race. These effects suggest a complicated web of diverse processes and factors, including, and with possible overlap:

1. The supply and, especially, demand for specific job occupants and the determinants of that supply and demand—the labor market processes that match men with jobs (see, e.g., Coleman et al., 1972:295–296)[3]

2. The changing social and economic utilities of diverse qualities, including minority-group membership, considered essential qualifications for various jobs

3. The cost and nature of on-the-job training, dependent in part on a job's technical complexity, its similarity to formal schooling, and the trainees' backgrounds

4. The specific use made of formal education by different jobs and the actual difference that varying the quality of education makes in the performance of specific jobs[4]

5. The extent of "credentialism," which one might cynically define as the private divorce of alleged job requirements from the actual job use of formal schooling, coupled with a public marriage between the possession of certain educational credentials and the right of access to specific jobs[5]

6. The related phenomenon by which some jobs' occupants "upgrade" the minimum credentials required for access to that job in order to enhance its expected earnings or social status, without regard for either the job relevance of higher credentials or their probable effect on the work productivity, job satisfaction, or relationships among differently qualified colleagues on the job[6]

7. The income inequality and income value difference of various resources that may result because different groups' members pay different prices for items of similar quality (e.g., education, housing, food; see Michelson, 1973:103–104)

8. The less directly economic, or purely noneconomic, functions of education—that is, its varied impact on consumer behavior, the ability to find and use public services, life styles, consumption of natural resources, political involvement, and the upbringing and informal education of children (see Michael, 1973)

Both theoretical models (to order and interrelate these processes) and statistical analyses (of education, job status, income, and other data) must be used simultaneously. Sociology's all-too-frequent separation of the larger issues in traditional social stratification theory from the descriptive results of recent empirical analyses of the socioeconomic life cycle is highly regrettable, as the controversy surrounding Coleman's and Jencks's works vividly illustrates.[7]

In this study, for example, we have referred to the qualities that seem causally related to personal income as "resources" that "produce" income (that is, have income value). This terminology implies a model of the school as a cultural factory that processes its occupants by adding value to the raw mental resources brought to the classrooms from diverse family backgrounds. The result is an unknown "output" worthy of certification (all evidence—or lack thereof—for the actual future uses of schooling aside). The simplistic view of education's effect on job status and income (see Chapter 7) is consonant with this model. Similar theoretical material is found in some economics literature. Two examples are the financial investment model of the human capital approach (Mincer, 1962, 1970; Hanoch, 1967; Chiswick, 1973) and the "wage competition" (Thurow, 1972)'theory of the labor market. In the latter, wages are set economically by supply and demand; job-relevant skills are instilled by formal schooling, among other processes. Wages then depend on the scarcity of these skills. Davis and Moore's (1945) stratification theory could be considered the sociological counterpart of this economic theory, given its picture of the production and distribution of scarce skills into variously demanding and "functionally important" jobs (Simpson, 1956).

However, there is also argument and evidence for a labor market theory (see Thurow, 1972; Jencks, 1973) in which wages are sociologically and historically set at "prevailing" levels *not* directly responsive to the supply of skills, much less their scarcity. Instead of wage competition, this theory focuses on "job competition" (see Thurow, 1972). When jobs are perceived as seeking the best available people at the prevailing wage, education is seen less as a culture factory instilling scarce skills and more as a certification agent for the fact that a person is "trainable" for various jobs.

In short, a clearer understanding of the diverse processes interconnecting education, training, job characteristics, income, and race requires greater use of more completely elaborated, alternative theoretical models together with empirical analyses designed to test those models. To achieve this convergence we need to develop correspondence rules that link theoretical models with empirical observations.

FINDINGS AND POLICY MAKING

The link between findings and policy making is generally considered self-evident. Too often, this judgment produces the kind of disputation that has surrounded the works of Coleman (1966), Jensen (1969), and Jencks (1972). Typically, the research findings have suggested that certain factors are more important constituents of IQ scholastic test scores, or status (job status and income level) than are other factors; the implication then drawn by authors or critics is that policy can henceforth afford to neglect the "unimportant" factors. Critics with vested interests in these factors (e.g., education) subsequently raise a storm of protest, while a puzzled lay public looks on.

At the roots of such intellectual conflicts are some basic methodological questions. First, precisely how do our estimates of the absolute and relative effects of different factors relate to policies that might possibly alter the conditional, marginal, or joint distributions, the means, variances, or ranges of each factor, in accordance with any stated goal? Second, how is the policy relevance of findings affected by the particular statistic chosen to measure the importance of various factors; the selection of the sample studied; the degree to which various factors can be manipulated by policy; and the degree to which theoretical development affects the research design, and precedes and controls the data analysis, as evident in the researchers' responses to problems involving identification and multicollinearity?

These unresolved issues have reappeared in each successive controversy. This is not the place either to illustrate that fact or to elaborate our position on these questions. However, one aspect is particularly relevant to our study. Central to recent disputes have been questions regarding the policy-making value of statistics focused on the percentage of variance explained by each of several factors (see, for example, Cain and Watts, 1970, Coleman, 1970, and Aigner, 1970, on Coleman et al., 1966; Bereiter, 1970, on Jensen, 1969; and Rivlin, 1973, and Thurow, 1973, on Jencks et al., 1972). The modest amounts of variance typically explained by individual factors or sets of factors have too often been the basis for simplistic, and sometimes unwarranted, policy suggestions (Cain and Watts, 1970) and wholesale challenges to the significance of sociological research (see, for example, Phillips, 1971; Hamblin, 1971). With some exceptions (among them Cain and Watts, 1970; Aigner, 1970; and Bereiter, 1970), critics too often share with authors an acceptance of the amount of variance explained as the unqualified criterion for determining scientific success.

As we note in Chapter 2, explained variance is but one measure of a variable's relative importance, and often not the most preferable one at that. There are different ways to implement the same goal (for example, equality for whites and blacks), and these have different statistical counterparts. From Cain and Watts (1970) and Bereiter (1970), we know that policies can be framed whose purpose is, variously, to increment the mean values of key variables, for example, those determining IQ or income; to change the degree to which such variables affect, say, IQ or income generally (that is, to change slopes); to change the variances and intercorrelations among the determinants of income, IQ, and so on; or to change the variances of income, IQ, and so on. The effect of policies that would alter means, variances, and slopes is suggested but not strictly evident in the values of these statistics, because the latter are empirically and theoretically contingent on a usually incomplete specification of the relationships influencing the factors we study. The theoretical contingency is illustrated, for example, in Michelson's comment (1973:98) on Jencks et al. that *if* some amount of income inequality is necessary, equalizing education may well cause some other institution to stratify the labor force and distribute people across incomes. As he put it, "if income inequality is in fact generated regardless of schooling, the present correlation between education and income is just a measure of the extent to which school is the institution *currently* used to distribute people among incomes" [our italics]. In short, as we suggested earlier, statistics of any sort will usually not imply any sharp, one-to-one correspondence between themselves and a single best policy.

Accordingly, we have been careful in the interpretation of the various standardized regression coefficients in our analysis. We are neither embarrassed nor self-congratulatory about the percentage of variance we usually explain (21 to 36 percent of income; 15 to 44 percent of job status). The relative determination of individuals' incomes by each resource is an interesting question in its own right, but *not* the most attractive measure of the relative importance of each. We therefore placed greater emphasis on decomposing average income differences, working essentially from another measure of relative importance: the general effect of a resource on income times its mean value, for groups of white and black graduates. We did so believing that the absolute effects of resources are more pertinent to black-white inequality than is the income variation for each group explained by these resources. We also believe that achieving equal results for racial groups would be a signal accomplishment from an equalitarian viewpoint, even though the individual incomes of black and white men are only modestly determined by these resources.

If we investigate further the relationship between component analyses and policy making, we need to ask: What economic and social policies determine the larger components in various analyses, and to what extent? In the absence of any policy changes, how stable are the various components and subcomponents related to each resource? What actually happens to various components after the implementation of policies designed to diminish or enlarge those components? Answering these questions requires moving beyond the hypothetical character of our regression slopes—for example, the change in Y that would result, hypothetically, from a unit change in X—to analyses of the degree to which subsequently observed changes correspond to hypothetical changes.

In conclusion, we propose two kinds of future research. Both would focus on black-white differences in the relationships among formal schooling, training, experience, job characteristics, and income. The first should be a national study of black and white college graduates of both sexes. At minimum this study should assess (1) the contribution of school quality to the economic fortunes of graduates; (2) the relative effect of schooling on the distribution of graduates to specific jobs, together with the income-value ranges of experience, graduate education, employment sector, and job status for alumni graduated from colleges of diverse quality levels, and located in different geographic regions; (3) the diverse self-selection processes of college entrants and graduates as a function of high-school performance, family background, race, and perhaps sex; (4) the components of average income differences, both for the country as a whole, and for graduates compared by residence, work place, employment sector, specific professions and jobs, and quality of undergraduate schooling; and (5) the effects of graduate and professional schooling, over and above that of undergraduate education.

The second would be a set of regional and local studies of blacks and whites, males and females, in specific occupational, educational, and employee groups. By carefully selecting such groups, the income-value ranges of specific resources could be estimated, and the functions of education, training, and experience for various jobs could be more easily assessed. For both analyses, more attention should be paid than has been in the past to the jobs held relative to the job holders' characteristics.

Finally, our study and other studies of status attainment among blacks and whites have virtually ignored the inequality of results for black and white women, and for men and women within each group. The former topic is particularly interesting, given the equality and even superiority (see Chapter 5) of well educated black women's incomes over those of comparable white women. Our understanding of discrimination will be seriously incomplete without an adequate explanation of this phenomenon as well as of differences between men and women of the same race.

NOTES

1.   The value of such studies is made vividly clear by Wohlstetter and Coleman (1970); see also Thurow (1970) and Chiswick and Mincer (1972).

2.   Such analyses have recently been mandated by some courts in connection with suits brought against civil service exams and other screening criteria, on grounds that they are job-irrelevant and discriminatory. Griggs v. Duke Power Co. (915 U.S. 849, March 8, 1971), a crucial Supreme Court decision, has been the basis for these mandates. For an example of such analyses, see Cohen and Chaiken (1972).

3.   See also Benham (1971:246–252). Coleman (1973), criticizing Jencks et al. (1972), has recently expressed a similar concern with the supply and demand for different occupations.

4.   Sharp (1970:97–111) showed that the prestige of undergraduate institutions affected the distribution of their alumni into specific jobs; it also affected graduates' incomes from specific jobs. *Except* for graduates in business and managerial positions, she found a "surprisingly low correspondence" between school prestige and earnings 5 years after graduation (1970:110).

5.   See, for example, Miller and Reissman (1969:69–77). Taubman and Wales (1973:43–49) recently estimated that up to 50 percent of the private returns of education may reflect the use of education as a screening device rather than as a provider of necessary skills.

6.   Under the rubric of "occupational licensing," some economists have discussed a variant of this phenomenon. From Rottenberg (1962) and Friedman (1962), it appears that such licensing (which encompasses barbers, beauty culturists, embalmers, physicians, nurses, pharmicists, plumbers, professional engineers, real estate brokers, and many other occupational groups) favors the "producers" of the services involved by raising the entry cost to applicants and thereby restricting access to the job (although the producers defend this practice as a "safeguard to consumers").

7.   The reason is that the policy significance of the empirical analyses are less clear than they could be. The absence of an explicit, theory-data link may provide momentary grist for critics' mills, but more crucially it creates an intellectual situation in which both the authors and especially the critics—who are understandably less familiar with the intricacies of the data—are likely to overinterpret the policy significance of the analyses. (See Jencks's second thoughts in responding to his critics, 1972:164.)

Appendix A

MATCHED SAMPLING_____

Again, methodology rears its ugly head. We did not begin with the intention of writing a treatise on methodology. . . The truth of the matter is, however, that many an issue ordinarily considered to fall exclusively within the providence of theory turns out to hinge on principles of methodology as soon as we consider how the issue could conceivably be resolved by empirical inquiry. We are, therefore, contending for a much more intimate relationship between theory and method than ordinarily has been contemplated, even by writers preoccupied with this particular interface between segments of the scientific quest.

BLAU and DUNCAN (1967:194–195)

SELF-SELECTION: AN ALTERNATIVE EXPLANATION

We first consider an important alternative explanation (to that presented above) of the observed gap between whites' and blacks' mean incomes. The self-selection processes discussed here would affect any study of college graduates, regardless of the research's sampling techniques, and is not a consequence of matched sampling. Nevertheless, we must consider the effect of this process on our results.

First, our matching ensured that the pairs of matched graduates had the same background, but could not control for the effect of socioeconomic background in determining *which* white and black students among secondary school classmates ultimately became college graduates. These students have surmounted at least three educational hurdles: high-school graduation, college admission, and college graduation. At each hurdle, whites and blacks alike face disqualification, whether from below-average academic abilities, disadvantaged social backgrounds, or other causes.

Since we have reason to believe that backgrounds and abilities are not equally distributed among whites and blacks, these events involve differential selection or elimination of whites and blacks. The result, at least in theory, is that among college graduates, background and academic ability should have a weaker relationship with postcollege achievement, that is, they should influence that achievement to a lesser extent, than would be the case for a

155

general sample of people at all educational levels. Similarly, we would expect social background and academic ability to influence postcollege achievement less for black than for white graduates. A concomitant result, ironically, is that we would also expect black graduates in our study to be more successful after college than white graduates, *if* the socioeconomic system places blacks in the same jobs as equally qualified whites and pays equal salaries for those jobs.

Let us consider the effect of socioeconomic background and academic ability at each of the three hurdles just mentioned; for the moment, our concern is with the men involved, without regard to race. First, we can safely hypothesize that students with less academic ability and lower socioeconomic status are less likely to graduate from high school. To be sure, some in these categories will graduate, but more will not. A similar hypothesis suggests that high-school graduates with lower academic ability and poorer backgrounds will enter college less frequently. Certainly some such graduates will matriculate, but they will probably differ in some way from students of similar ability and background who failed to graduate from high school or, having graduated, failed to enter college. Furthermore, the success of such graduates suggests that we should entertain some doubts about the strength of these variables as determinants of whether a student will complete college.

Indeed, we know that some students with less academic ability and poorer backgrounds *will* graduate despite these continued disadvantages. However, the effects of these disadvantages should be even less than at previous points in the path toward college graduation. Students from disadvantaged backgrounds who have survived to this point, it might be argued, should now be more likely to graduate than their equally disadvantaged colleagues were to surmount previous hurdles. Whatever the unknown characteristics that cause this strength, those students who graduate should be even more different from their high-school contemporaries than were the other disadvantaged students who succeeded only in graduating from high school or entering college. Furthermore, by this time the preponderance of students left in the educational stream are from above-average backgrounds and have above-average academic abilities, relative to their high-school classmates. The more severe the selection processes at previous stages, and/or the greater the influence of academic ability and background on the chances of graduating from high school, and so forth, the greater the extent to which this condition exists.

We now consider a final hurdle—"making it" in postcollege life. First, we would still expect the more able and advantaged students to have a better chance for graduation and success than their less able and less advantaged classmates. However, at this point it is unlikely that early disadvantages will greatly alter the postcollege success of the less advantaged, because such students have long exercised qualities such as determination and ambition to offset those disadvantages, and presumably will continue to do so. (To be sure, the more academically difficult the schools the students have passed through, the greater will be the attrition of disadvantaged students, and the more other qualities will have had to offset the disadvantages of those who survive.) Overall, the effects of background and ability on college graduates' postcollege success should not be as great as on the success of groups within the general population (without regard to educational level).

Another important background factor is race. However, as in the discussion above, we would argue that blacks who have managed to graduate from college despite socioeconomic and other disadvantages have probably compensated for those disadvantages. Thus we expect that the effects on success of being black would be less for them than for blacks in general. Furthermore, blacks are generally "selected out" to a greater degree than whites. Therefore, the combined effects on success of poor family background and less-than-average academic ability should be less for blacks than for whites. The net result might be that black college graduates would do a little better than white graduates after college if there are no other factors, such as discrimination at work. This conclusion requires the "other" qualities to be perceived as a kind of hidden advantage that enters the picture as one result of the selection process. Although it may well be true for specific individuals, this conclusion probably does not hold generally.

The more likely, if conservative, conclusion is that blacks who survive the selection process are probably doing better than all blacks, and certainly better than those who dropped out earlier. The same kind of statement could be made about whites who survive the selection process, though it would probably be true to a lesser degree. However, it does not follow necessarily that the success of surviving black graduates will be greater than that of surviving whites, even though the selection process has probably narrowed the success gap at each hurdle along the way.

These possibilities have implications for matched sampling. We can devise a comparison of whites and blacks equal in ability and background through matched sampling or an analogous real social process (e.g., in a parallel sense, black and white athletes selected by major league teams have been matched with respect to ability). Given such an equation on nominal prerequisites, Negroes *may* ultimately be more successful than whites because in addition to their matched abilities and backgrounds, they possess other characteristics that have compensated for the disadvantages that eliminated many of their contemporaries along the way. At minimum, though, the gap between whites' and blacks' success has been narrowed, if not erased, by the selection process.[1]

We now consider some implications of this line of reasoning. If we match graduates of the most demanding schools according to ability and background and then examine the difference between blacks' and whites' incomes, we would expect the difference between the elites to be smaller than that between blacks and whites in general. Such income gaps normally favor whites, but in this particular case we might even expect blacks to overtake whites. However, if black students from poor families receive substantial scholarship assistance that prevents them from being selected out of college for financial reasons, the selection process will be altered or overshadowed, and the degree of its responsibility for black-white differences in postcollege successes would thus be altered. Black graduates might do better, the same, or worse than white graduates for reasons having to do with factors other than those resulting from the hypothesized selection process just discussed.

As we have seen, blacks' more severe self-selection process has probably narrowed the success gap for black and white graduates, in contrast to blacks and whites generally. It is sadly ironic that if this process were to become less severe for blacks—perhaps no more severe for blacks than for whites—the income gap between college graduates of both races might be even greater than it is. On balance, then, insofar as we interpret part or all of the income gap as the result of discrimination and other factors, we will err in a conservative direction, if at all. Thus the general selection process just described does not constitute an invalidating factor, in the way that selection can invalidate experiments carried out in a laboratory setting. It is rather an alternative, substantive explanation for part of the observed differences in black and white graduates' success (e.g., mean incomes).

MATCHED SAMPLING AND ITS DRAWBACKS

We now consider the difficulties in our sampling method. Although its use seems to be declining because of an increased awareness of its hazards, matched sampling has been almost a methodological cliché in educational research. Its traditional strength has been the intuitive appeal of equalizing matched groups with respect to one or more variables.

Typically, researchers are most interested in the effects of a dichotomous variable that might be termed "experimental group-control group," or, as in our case, "one natural group (black)-another natural group (white)." To take an experimental example, a psychologist might study the effect of democratic versus authoritarian teaching methods on the intelligence quotients (IQ's) of school children. IQ would be a *dependent variable*, since it depends on the way classrooms are conducted. The variable of central interest—which we might term the "political climate" of education, as manifested in two varieties of classroom teaching—we call the *match* variable. In our study, the match variable is obviously race. The other variables on which the two or more groups are explicitly matched are called the *matching variables*; for example, children in the two types of classrooms might be matched or paired off with respect to their fathers' educational levels of their IQ scores from earlier years. Within graduation years, our black and white graduates were paired off with respect to two matching variables: grade-point average and father's job status. As a result of this matching, the relationship in the general population between the match variable and matching variables is eliminated in the matched samples, to the extent that the matching is perfect.

In experimental research, matched sampling is more useful when accompanied by a random selection of the people who comprise the matched groups. Such randomization has the effect of equalizing matched pairs of people with respect to other external or extraneous variables not specified among the dependent, match, or matching variables.

In quasi- or nonexperimental settings, the case with this study, people cannot be randomly selected to membership in one or another natural group. Therefore, we could only randomize the choice of which Negro or white graduates would be studied. Such randomization does nothing to equalize black and white graduates on external variables and, hence, did not eliminate the relationship in the matched sample between the match (race) and the external variables. However, it increased the probability that these relationships, however strong or weak, probably represented accurately the relationships in a larger population of all white and black graduates from our three schools. This fact facilitated assessment of the importance of the external variables that we measured, and we used appropriate statistical controls in doing so.

The basic analysis of matched samples is a comparison of their dependent variables' means. For example, we compared the mean income differences between black and white college graduates. However, before drawing an inference that the differences found were indeed a function of the match variable (here, racial differences), we wanted to ascertain that they had not resulted, instead, from limitations on the initial sample, attrition, imperfect matching, spurious relationships, and regression to the mean. These possibilities are discussed below, after a description of our data.

THE DATA

The college graduates surveyed were drawn from three universities located in the eastern United States. To preserve their anonymity, we gave them fictitious names: Atlantic State University (ASU), Metropolitan State University (MSU), and Frazier University. The last is attended primarily by blacks; the others are integrated universities attended predominantly by whites.

The survey was done in three stages. First, all available ASU and MSU blacks who were graduated in the years 1931 to 1964 were interviewed by the National Opinion Research Center (NORC). Second, we constructed two lists, one of ASU and MSU white graduates who were classmates[2] of the previously interviewed black graduates, and one of Frazier University black graduates. Briefly, the first list was comprised of a series of simple or systematic random samples of white graduates in each class, and also included black graduates already interviewed. Usually, 10 to 20 whites were listed for every black. The second list was also a random sample within classes, except that, for some classes, we included all graduates for whom we could obtain addresses. Finally, from the first list (2420 ASU and 3200 MSU whites), we interviewed and analyzed data on 126 ASU and 200 MSU whites; from the second (1638 black Frazier graduates), we interviewed 276.

Ideally, for each black graduate of ASU and MSU interviewed in the first stage of our study, we found in the second list a white who had graduated from his school in the same year, with the same background as measured by the job status of his father or head of household[3] and with the same grade-point average; and a black Frazier graduate who had also graduated in the same year, had the same background, and the same grade-point average. If more than one person in either list matched a particular MSU or ASU black graduate in these respects, we randomly selected only one to be interviewed. The Frazier graduates chosen to match the ASU blacks were termed "Frazier–1"; those who matched the MSU blacks became "Frazier–2." When the interviews were completed, we had matches as specified for virtually all of the previously interviewed ASU and MSU blacks. For practical reasons the ideal procedures were not always followed, but the original point of the matched sampling was largely served: We equated groups of white and black graduates in terms of graduation year, grades, and father's job status. Various statistical techniques, such as regression standardization, were used to neutralize the minimal differences that remained.

While the Frazier graduates were explicitly matched to ASU and MSU black graduates, we were more interested in comparing Frazier–1 and Frazier–2 graduates with the ASU and MSU white groups respectively, even though the individual Frazier graduates were matched to these white graduates only indirectly, by virtue of their common match to individual ASU or MSU blacks. (Pairs matched indirectly are not ordinarily as similar to one another as pairs matched directly; see the following discussion of the quality of all matches.) The matching process produced four groups of matched graduates: (1) ASU white and black classmates, (2) MSU white and black classmates, (3) ASU white and Frazier–1 black graduates, and (4) MSU white and Frazier–2 black graduates.[4] Occasionally, we combined the Frazier–1 and –2 groups and compared the whole Frazier group to the combined group of MSU and ASU white graduates.[5]

THE QUALITY OF THE DATA

Several factors can affect the quality of both the data and the analysis of matched samples. We first examine factors limiting the samples interviewed.

LIMITATIONS ON INITIAL SAMPLES

We began by listing all graduates identified both as blacks and as graduates of ASU or MSU from 1930 through 1964. Since neither school kept student records by race, we examined the pictures of seniors in the colleges' yearbooks. In doing so we may have missed as many as 10 percent of the black graduates. While speculation to the contrary is possible, we doubt that this percent differed significantly in their characteristics from the blacks whom we identified and interviewed.

Table A.1 shows that we located 184 graduates of ASU and 302 from MSU. Of these, we were unable to locate addresses for 10 percent.[6] Some whose addresses were available lived outside the middle Atlantic region of the United States and/or outside other areas of the country into which NORC could send interviewers. Larger percentages (20 to 30 percent) of the other three samples either had no address or lived outside the interviewing areas. Since losses from these three samples were randomly replaced, the only serious

TABLE A.1 GRADUATES' AVAILABILITY AND RESPONSE TO INTERVIEWERS, BY SAMPLE

	ASU Blacks		MSU Blacks		ASU Whites		MSU Whites		Frazier Blacks	
	(N)	(%)	(N)	(%)	(N)	(%)	(N)	(%)	(N)	(%)
Total ever considered for interviews	184		302		292		388		489	
I. Interviews not sought	18		31		92		90		108	
A. No address	14		26		27		20		51	
B. Outside NORC's interviewing areas	4		5		65		70		57	
II. Interviews requested of NORC	166	100	271	100	200	100	298	100	381	100
A. Not obtained[a]	39	24	71	26	49	24	77	26	100	26
1. Outright refusals[b]	18	46	43	61	17	35	34	44	23	23
2. Bad addresses; unable to[b] obtain appointment for interview	21	54	28	39	32	65	43	56	77	77
B. Interviews completed[a]	127	76	200	74	151	76	221	74	281	74
1. Interviews matched[c]	127	100	200	100	126	83	200	90	276	98
2. Interviews not used in[c] matches	0	0	0	0	25	17	21	10	5	2

[a] Percents are based on numbers of interviews requested.
[b] Percents are based on number of interviews not obtained.
[c] Percents are based on number of interviews completed.

162

consequence to the research is the likelihood that graduates living outside the middle Atlantic area were underrepresented in the sample (a graduate chosen at random to replace one who lived outside this region was more likely to be living within this region).

We eventually requested interviews of 166 ASU and 271 MSU black graduates. Of these, we could not obtain interviews for 24 percent of the ASU blacks and 26 percent of the MSU blacks because the graduates either refused to be interviewed when located, or could never be located, even with addresses. Similar percentages of the other samples were also unobtainable.

ATTRITION

Of the interviews actually obtained, some were eventually discarded because the interviewees proved not to match the other graduates after all.[7] The bottom line of Table A.1 shows that matches were found for virtually all of the origi-nally interviewed black ASU and MSU graduates. Discards were greatest for white ASU graduates: 17 percent of the total completed were not used in matches. The corresponding percentages for MSU white and Frazier University black graduates were 10 and 2 percent, respectively.

IMPERFECT MATCHING

Another factor that can affect matched samples is imperfect matching (see Althauser and Rubin, 1970). Not every ASU or MSU black graduate had both a white classmate *and* a black graduate from Frazier as acceptable matches, nor did every white graduate necessarily have a match in both the ASU or MSU black sample and the Frazier sample. Of 127 ASU black graduates, 126 were matched to white ASU graduates, and 127 to Frazier–1 graduates. Of the 155 black MSU graduates, 155 were matched to white MSU graduates, but only 149 to Frazier–2 graduates. The result was a combined Frazier sample of 276 (149 + 127) individuals implicitly matched to white ASU and MSU graduates, and 281 (155 + 126) explicitly matched to ASU and MSU black graduates. In addition, the matches that were made were not always perfect; that is, within graduation years, individual black and white graduates did not always (or even ordinarily) have identical grade-point averages or fathers with identical job-status scores.

Respondents versus Nonrespondents. One question that such data must al-ways raise is whether graduates not interviewed, the nonrespondents, for

whatever reason differ in any important respects from those who were interviewed and matched. Table A.2 shows data for both groups on grade-point
average and father's job status. The table shows, first, that in every sample,
the nonrespondents had higher averages than the respondents; however, the
size of the differences never exceeded .09 grade points and can thus be deemed
negligible.

Our initial data from the schools' files on the jobs of ASU and MSU black
graduates' fathers was of poor quality. Practically speaking, it was impossible
to code fathers' jobs using the Duncan index, so only Census categories were
used to code them. In addition, we had only a few of these graduates relative to
Frazier black graduates and white graduates—hence our decision to interview
ASU and MSU black graduates first. Table A.2 shows that the differences in
mean (census) categories between the respondent and the nonrespondent
groups ranged from .70 to .90, when we treat the numbers assigned to these
categories as roughly indicating job-status units. In general, non respondents'
fathers had higher-status jobs. The differences shown, while not negligible, are
not particularly serious. Furthermore, even if tests of statistical significance

TABLE A.2   MEAN GRADE-POINT AVERAGE AND FATHER'S OCCUPATION
OF RESPONDENTS AND NONRESPONDENTS, BY SAMPLE

	ASU Blacks	MSU Blacks	ASU Whites	MSU Whites	Frazier Blacks
Mean grade-point average[a]					
Respondents in matched sample	2.75	2.58	2.64	2.60	2.66
Nonrespondents[b]	2.74	2.50	2.57	2.56	2.57
Father's job status[c]					
Respondents in matched sample	5.41	5.05	29.5	31.9	27.6
Nonrespondents[b]	4.58	4.31	26.6	28.9	29.5

[a] 1 = A; 2 = B; 3 = C; 4 = D; 5 = F.

[b] Includes potential respondents outside of NORC interviewing areas, respondents
with no addresses available or with bad addresses, respondents refusing to be
interviewed, and others.

[c] For ASU and MSU blacks, we used Census categories: 1 = professional, technical,
and related occupations; 2 = managers, officials, and proprietors; 3 = sales;
4 = clerical; 5 = craftsmen, foremen, and related occupations; 6 = operatives
(semiskilled); 7 = service; 8 = unskilled and farm workers. For the three remaining groups, we use Duncan's socioeconomic index.

were appropriate here (and they are not), the differences would not be significant. More important, the relative status level of most clerical and craft occupations (coded with the numbers 4 and 5, respectively) as measured here is rather difficult to establish; to note just one ambiguity, many craft occupations bring higher incomes than many clerical jobs. In short, it is not clear that the numbers assigned to the Census categories constitute a steadily increasing, monotonic, ordinal, job-status scale.

For the remaining three samples, fathers' jobs were coded using Duncan's socioeconomic status index. On this measure, the fathers of white ASU and MSU nonrespondents appear to have jobs of slightly lower status than do the fathers of respondents. The opposite holds for Frazier graduates' fathers. Another difficulty is that some of the Duncan-index figures, as well as some of those based on Census categories, are not strictly comparable. "Father's job" for many nonrespondents referred to the job held by the father *while the graduate was in school.* However, fathers' jobs for all respondents were determined through our interviews with graduates and were the fathers' "primary occupation," which was sometimes different from the job they held during their sons' college years. If the job data for fathers were comparable, the average job status of nonrespondents' fathers would probably have been slightly greater than our data show.

Overall, then, we found no important differences between the two groups on either grade-point average or father's job status. We can infer from these findings, in turn, that there are no important differences between respondents and nonrespondents with respect to other factors that correlate highly with either grades or father's job status.[8]

Matching Procedures. As noted earlier, we did not always achieve *ideal* matches. First, as far as possible, matched graduates were selected for matching by graduation year; when impossible, we matched within 2 or 3 years of the same graduation date. Second, in practice, we defined +.60 grade-point units and +16 father's job-status units as acceptable differences between potential matches. It was not always possible to find matches within these limits, but considerable effort was made to do so. Finally, the matching was done according to a random procedure (described in Althauser and Rubin, 1970).[9]

Table A.3 presents data on our use of the four matching procedures. The data show that we were better able to observe the acceptable limits on grade-point average and randomizing than those on graduation year and father's job status. When we began the matching process, we had been willing to trade off

TABLE A.3 MATCHES ACCOMPLISHED IN ACCORDANCE WITH THE
PROCEDURES FOR RANDOMIZATION AND MATCHING, BY SAMPLE

	Samples Being Matched to ASU and MSU Black Graduates		
	ASU Whites (%)	MSU Whites (%)	Frazier Blacks (%)
Matched by all four procedures	74	77	80
Matched within acceptable limits on			
Cumulative grade average	94	94	94
Father's job status	88	92	93
Matched on year of graduation	88	90	93
Matched by the rules of randomization	98	93	98

poor matching on grades in order to obtain better matching on father's job status, which we considered the more important of the two matching variables. We therefore set rather wide acceptable limits (+.60) for grade matching. Even so, it still proved slightly more difficult to match father's job status than to match grade-point average. Overall, when we compare the percentages for the individual procedures with those for the four procedures together, we find that violations of more than one procedure were rather infrequent. We also see that, except for ASU whites, each procedure was observed at least 90 percent of the time.

Differences Eliminated by Matching.   The percentages in Table A.3 tell us only about the number of matches that exceeded our maximum acceptable difference. We still need to know how close the final differences were. We noted earlier that by matching we hoped to equalize black and white graduates with respect to grades and father's job status. Table A.4 shows the proportion of the differences in grades and father's job status that was eliminated by matching. For example, consider the difference of 17.4 in the fathers' job-status units for MSU white and black graduates. Using Duncan's socioeconomic index, we estimate that the mean job status of all MSU white fathers was 45.6;[10] for the blacks, 28.2. For the matched MSU white graduates, however, the corresponding figure is 31.9—78 percent (13.8/17.5) of the original difference (17.4 units). Similarly, 75 and 83 percent of the job-status differences were eliminated in the ASU white/black and ASU–MSU/Frazier matched samples, respectively. The differences in grade-point averages before matching were generally smaller than were fathers' job-status differences. For ASU graduates, the difference was negligible (−.03), and over 90 percent of the differences in the remaining two matched samples were eliminated by matching.

Table A.4 also shows that ASU and MSU whites in general had slightly higher average grades and fathers with higher job status than did the three black groups. When we examine data on job status from a national random sample of whites and blacks, we find the mean father's job status to be 34 and 19, respectively (Duncan, 1969). It thus appears that the fathers of our white and black graduates respectively have an average job status 9 to 12 units greater than that of fathers in Duncan's sample. Finally, Table A.4 shows that our indirect matches were at least as good as our direct ones.

Since there have been no prior studies comparable to ours in size and procedure, it is difficult to evaluate our own performance. However, it appears that nonrespondents do not differ significantly from respondents, that the

TABLE A.4 AMOUNT OF DIFFERENCE ELIMINATED ON MATCHING VARIABLES FOR THREE PAIRS OF MATCHED POPULATIONS

	Matched groups		
	ASU Whites ASU Blacks	MSU Whites MSU Blacks	ASU and MSU Whites Frazier Blacks
Mean grade-point average[a]			
Estimated mean for all white[b] graduates	2.64	2.37	2.49
Mean for matched whites	2.64	2.60	2.62
Mean for matched blacks	2.67	2.62	2.60
Proportion of difference eliminated in matching	0%	92%	118%[c]
Mean father's job status[d]			
Estimated mean for all white graduates	46.7	45.6	46.1
Mean for matched whites	29.5	31.9	30.8
Mean for matched blacks	23.9	28.2	27.6
Proportion of difference eliminated in matching	75%	78%	83%

[a] 1 = A; 2 = B; 3 = C; 4 = D; 5 = F.

[b] All whites ever considered for matching. There is no corresponding category for blacks, because both whites and Frazier blacks were matched to prechosen ASU and MSU blacks.

[c] Matching overcorrected the previous difference.

[d] Using Duncan's socioeconomic index.

procedures for constructing ideal matches were followed within practical limits, and that matching produced considerable, though not complete, equalization of black and white graduates. Finally, we discarded a far smaller proportion of cases than have researchers in many previous matched sample studies.

SPURIOUS RELATIONSHIPS

A third hazard of matched sampling has the effect of rendering spurious part of the inferred relationship between the match and dependent variables.[11] For example, there might be an external variable labeled "need to achieve" (n-ach) for which we had no measures. N-ach might be associated with race; for example, black graduates might have more n-ach than whites. It might also influence the incomes earned by black and white graduates. As a result, part of the apparent effect of race on incomes might rather by caused by the two facts that n-ach influences income and is associated with race. This spurious component in the relationship between race and income may be positive or negative, that is, it may spuriously enlarge or decrease the apparent relationship between race and income, depending on the positive or negative character of the relationships between n-ach and income, n-ach and race, and race and income. For example, if we assume that (1) the greater the n-ach, the greater the income, (2) whites have higher mean incomes than blacks, and (3) blacks have more n-ach than whites, then the relationship between race and income will be misleadingly small. We would have to make a statistical adjustment for n-ach before we could discover the "real" (larger, in this case) income differences between white and black graduates.

In actual research, the seriousness of the difficulties posed by spurious relationships largely depends on the substantive theories held by either a researcher or his critics. One or the other usually theorizes that certain variables are likely or unlikely to create spurious components in the relationship between the match and the dependent variables.[12] For our part, we hypothesized that no omitted variables, with the possible exception of IQ, were likely to create a spurious component in the relationship between race and graduates' incomes.

REGRESSION TO THE MEAN

Perhaps the most infamous hazard for matching has been "regression to the mean." Because of it, part or all of a difference between the means of two matched groups on a dependent variable—for example, our gap in mean incomes for blacks and whites—may be artifactual. Several explanations for this result can be found in the methodological literature. First, it arises because the groups selected for study show extreme values on some variable. For example, groups may receive remedial treatment after showing very poor test scores. Second, it reflects imperfect correlations between pretreatment and posttreatment measures, for example, between test scores preceding and following remedial treatment. Third, in addition to reflecting imperfect correlation, it is linked to that part of the correlation that reflects imperfect measures. Thus, test scores can reflect not only what student actually knows but also his luck or previous night's sleep.

These explanations apply to this study in the following ways. The matched graduates from Frazier (all blacks) and the integrated schools (all whites) were selected because their fathers had jobs with the atypically low status needed to match that of the fathers of black MSU and ASU graduates (see above discussion of respondents' and nonrespondents' characteristics). Also, in some instances the grade-point averages of ASU and MSU blacks were slightly lower than those of whites. In addition, our data certainly show imperfect correlations between father's job status and/or grades, and graduates' personal incomes. Finally, one could argue that measurement error has affected all three of these variables, although such an error in income, as a dependent— that is, posttreatment—variable, could not contribute to regression effects.

Althauser and Rubin (1971) and Barnow (1972:6) have developed similar equations for estimating the contribution of measurement error in father's job status to the gap in graduates' incomes.

According to either equation, the actual regression effect is a product of three factors: the difference in black and white graduates' fathers' average job status in the unmatched population, the absolute effect (regression coefficient) of father's job status on income, and the amount of measurement error in father's job status. Regarding the first of these, approximately 10 and 20 units of status separate Frazier and white ASU and MSU graduates from black ASU and MSU graduates, respectively. Thus, the first factor is large. Second, there are two sets of estimates for the effect of father's job status on graduates' incomes from which we can choose a figure to represent absolute effect. In a general, that is, not necessarily college-educated population of black and white men, Duncan (1969) found that this effect was zero for blacks, and .02 for whites. An increase of 1 unit in father's job status corresponded to an increment of .02 × $1000, or $20, for example. We could utilize this estimate for whites with some confidence if we knew that it did not depend on the level of education received by their sons. However, our arguments regarding self-selection (see beginning of Appendix A) imply a weaker effect of father's job status on graduates' incomes than would hold for men generally. In our own data (Table 3.1) we found negative effects for our white graduates and small positive coefficients (.00, .01, .02, .07) for our black graduates. These may or may not be the same coefficients as would be estimated from data for the total population of graduates from our three universities. How do we choose between these estimates?

If the appropriate coefficient is zero (which, incidentally, is the near average of all the coefficients just cited), there is no regression effect no matter what the measurement error in father's job status. But to be very conservative, let us use .02. We then need to examine the possible sources of measurement error. Coding error is one possible source, but an independent recoding of 100 respondents' fathers' job statuses revealed too small an error to produce any effect. Let us guess that for any of several other reasons, there is an average absolute error of +8 status units (a fairly large amount) in our coefficients. In that case the resulting contribution of the regression artifact to the income gaps (for details, see Althauser and Rubin, 1971) is $130 for differences involving ASU and MSU blacks, and $65 for those involving Frazier blacks. These are small relative to the differences we found in the data (from $1200 to $2700 in 1966 dollars), and we therefore chose to ignore them; the correction for inflation reduces the income gap more than does any regression effect.

Because of the small differences in grade-point averages and the virtual absence of measurement error in them, we presumed no regression effect from grades.[13] However, if we assume a rather poor reliability (say, .25) for grades as we have used them, the largest regression effect that we can come up with is still less than $175.[14]

One possible source of artifact remains: imperfect correlation per se between grades or father's job status, and income. Our discussion of measurement error covered part of this possibility. We therefore confine ourselves here to noting the effects of an imperfect correlation between income and error-free measures of grades or job status. Despite assertions to the contrary (Campbell and Clayton, 1961; Campbell and Stanley, 1966; and Campbell and Erlebacher, 1971), such correlations *do not* create any part of the mean income differences estimated from matched samples.[15]

OTHER ISSUES

As this study progressed, some methodological issues arose concerning the conduct of this survey, the nature of our data, and the status of its analysis.

These were first prompted by the fact that our data are drawn from graduates of only three schools, all located in the East. By anyone's common-sense notion of Gallup polling, our sample, containing as it does 600 blacks and 300 whites, seems unrepresentative and otherwise inadequate. From such a sample one certainly could not estimate the mean incomes of all black and white graduates, or the percentage of all graduates who would, say, have voted for Richard Nixon in 1972. The question thus becomes: To whom can we generalize, and is the group to which we can generalize of any particular interest? The underlying issue, of course, is whether we ought to represent our findings as anything other than descriptive of our particular sample. Most researchers using broader, more representative samples have interpreted their results as estimates of general relationships among variables, that is, as "laws." However, are such samples necessary if one wishes to make such general interpretations?

The apparent answer seems affirmative, but there are several related arguments against it. The first is exemplified in Zetterberg's contention (1965) that a distinction must be made between "descriptive" and "verification" studies: only the former require representative samples. "The relationships expressed in the theoretical propositions are presumed to be universally present. They are accordingly, present both in representative and in non-representative samples. To disprove or demonstrate their existence is, hence, possible in any kind of sample—biased or unbiased" (1965; 128–129). Zetterberg goes on to qualify his position, in part: "When using a biased sample for a verification, we must have assurance that the relationship we want to prove is not introduced into our data by selective sampling. . . . Also, when using a biased sample for verification, we should realize that we have no knowledge of the population to which the result can be safely generalized" (1965:129).

Blalock (1968:192–196) has elaborated a similar line of reasoning, in particular arguing a similar distinction between generalizing to "laws" and generalizing to populations. His basic point is that the hazard to inferences about lawlike relationships among variables results less from the representativeness of the sample than from one's theoretical argument that all relevant variables have been included in the system under study—that is, the "populations are closed". Moreover, we would add that, in general, estimates of variable relationships cannot be interpreted *without* reference to the research design's ability to mitigate the effects of extraneous variables on the relationships under study. In our view, the most important question in evaluating such estimates is whether their foundation in a single or special, that is, nonrepresentative, population will be misleading as a result of the effects of (1) uncontrolled methodological or substantive variables or (2) theoretical variables not included in research design.

Another issue begins by underscoring researchers' perennial trade-off between the ability to generalize and the ability to control for alternative methodological explanations of findings (i.e., achieving "external" versus "internal" validity of hypotheses; see Wiggins, 1968: 390–392). A principle purpose of research design is to restrict the impact of extraneous factors on tests of hypotheses. Matching, randomizing, and sometimes even eliminating variation on certain variables (Wiggins, 1968) are well-known ways to achieve this goal. We have already discussed matching and randomizing in this study. In order to eliminate some variation, we excluded female graduates and males graduating later than 1964. Including either or both would have obviously increased the generalizability of our study and made it more representative. The same result would have followed had we included colleges from other regions, and/or with a greater range in the quality of education offered.

However, each of these additional factors would have increased the potential explanations of findings. That is, we might have found ourselves accounting for mean income differences in terms of differences in the proportions of female, as against male, black and white college graduates; or of educational quality at black, in contrast to white, schools. The greater the number of such factors, the more difficult it becomes to study any one particular explanation, hypothesis, or limited set of hypotheses. By ruling out females and virtually eliminating variation in the quality of education, we were able to concentrate on other possible explanations. While some social scientists place greater emphasis on generalizability than on control of extraneous variation, our view (and that of Campbell and Stanley, 1966; and Wiggins, 1968) is that the latter has greater importance than the former. The best design, of course, would maximize both, but when we cannot have both in equal measure, the latter has priority.

As both Blalock and Zetterberg have suggested, one does not generalize (to larger populations) estimates based on samples as limited as ours. Yet many of the restrictions on our sample—the lack of variation in educational quality, the very modest variation in graduates' region of present residence, the all-male sample—provided implicit controls that would otherwise have to have been introduced by statistical means. As a result, even before statistical controls were applied, our estimates of relationships took several extraneous variables into account. Therefore, when additional controls, such as using partial regression analysis and standardization were applied in combination with those already implicit in the design and sample, the resulting relationships among variables should have been estimates of the general, lawlike relationships among these variables. Thus we generalized to laws and not to real populations.

Of course, it does not follow that the same variable relationships will necessarily hold when the mean values of the extraneous variables are different, as might be the case if our sample had been drawn from three schools in the South, or from three schools offering education of higher or lower quality than the three we chose (though a reasonable starting hypothesis would be that the relationships would hold across all such values). Whether the lawlike relationships estimated from our data *are* the same would then depend on whether interaction occurs between region or educational quality and these relationships. If it does, then we must conclude that different laws operate within different regions or quality-groupings; our findings would, therefore, be less general than we had thought when we presumed no interaction. A national sample might provide estimates of more laws, such as those that hold within different levels of variables like region or quality (as in a study of low, moderate, high and very high quality, for example). This situation can affect the generalizability of results from any type of study.

For perspective, we could compare the results from analyzing a hypothetical, national, representative sample with those from our own sample, assuming that the same variables are similarly studied. Before controlling for region or quality of education, either or both may account for part of the relationships found in a national sample. However, once region and quality of education are controlled (if possible), then the resulting estimates should be identical to ours *if* there is no statistical interaction between region or quality and the relationships under study. If such interaction exists, say, with respect to region, then analysis of the representative sample should be confined to each region in turn; the resulting estimates for the eastern region should then be close to ours. Likewise, if there is interaction between quality of education *and* region, then estimates from the representative sample that are based on high quality schools in the eastern region should produce estimates similar to ours. The common difficulty with national samples under such circumstances is that such regional analyses and categories of educational quality rarely include a sufficient number of cases. It is even more unlikely that a national sample would include enough cases to enable analyses of these two variables simultaneously, and an inadequate case base has severe consequences for the statistical quality (probability of type I and II errors) of the estimated relationships.

In sum, the generalizability of our estimates to other populations depends on whether statistical interaction occurs or does not occur. However, our estimates *are* estimates of lawlike relationships and are thus of interest to any study of this topic, regardless of interaction between variables. The eastern region has been an important area of black settlement and employment, and an above-average quality of education is offered by the colleges in this sample. The black graduates from these schools are certainly an elite among all black college graduates and, hence, among all blacks. To a lesser extent, the white graduates are also member of an elite. Ironically, the very fact that they are unrepresentative makes them a crucial group on which to examine matters of theory and policy. If *our* black graduates cannot "make it" in postcollege life at least as well as matching white graduates, the promise of education seems empty indeed.

NOTES

1.   Of course, if we equalized *all* the relevant characteristics of whites and blacks, such as determination, ambition, ability, and background where relevant, we could expect no black superiority in subsequent athletic or occupational performance.

2.   As used in this research, "class," "classes," and "classmates" always refer to year of graduation and not (as is sometimes the case in universities) to class year as established by year of matriculation.

3.   In a few cases, the respondent's father was not present in the home during the time the graduate attended college. In such cases we substituted data on the mother or other head of household rather than drop the respondent from the sample.

4.   Since both Frazier subgroups are totally black, we often refer to them simply as Frazier–1 and Frazier–2 graduates, with no reference to race.

5.   We also gathered data on 55 MSU white and black graduates who received 2-year Associate of Arts (A.A.) degrees. These data are not discussed in this book.

6.   We searched for addresses in the schools' alumni files and in the motor vehicle bureau files of the states in which the schools were located.

7.   This process, which we termed "attrition," further reduces the sample size and can increase the unrepresentative character of the final sample to an often unnecessary and objectionable degree. The percentage of cases discarded in the history of matched sampling has sometimes been as high as 96 percent.

8.   It should be noted, however, that there might be differences on other factors—those *not* highly correlated with either variable.

9.   All the ASU and MSU black respondents and potential matching graduates were assigned random numbers by group. As far as possible, we assigned each ASU or MSU black graduate to the lowest numbered white classmate and Frazier black graduate who also satisfied the other matching criteria (grade-point average, etc.). Likewise, when two or more ASU or MSU blacks matched a white graduate equally well, the black with the lowest random number was chosen for the match.

10.   This figure and those for ASU white and Frazier University graduates were based largely on school file data or a large (2400 from ASU; 3200, MSU; and 1600, Frazier) random sample of

white or black graduates for years in which the previously interviewed ASU and MSU blacks graduated. These data were available for about two-thirds of the ASU and MSU white graduates, and for 87 percent of the Frazier graduates. However, as was noted earlier, the job listed on college records was not necessarily the same as the father's primary occupation; the latter constituted the basis for matching.

11.   This hazard is labeled "self-selection" in the methodological literature (Campbell and Stanley, 1966). To avoid confusion with the discussion at the beginning of this Appendix and in order to explain the nature of the hazard (that is, the creation of spurious correlations), we chose to avoid Campbell and Stanley's term.

12.   Ordinary survey research not utilizing matched sampling is just as vulnerable to the unrevealed operation of variables external to a given researcher's theoretical system.

13.   Of course, had we used grades to indicate, say, mental ability or IQ, they would be subject to such error.

14.   The largest difference in average grades—.25—is that observed between MSU white and black graduates. The average effect of grades on their incomes is about .75. A reliability of .25 corresponds to a measurement error term (in Althauser and Rubin's equation 9) of .75. The product of these three numbers is $169.

15.   Let us consider a hypothetical matched sample constructed from two identical and symmetrical distributions of values for some perfectly measured pretreatment variable, X (say, father's job status), in which the means of the values differ prior to matching the two groups. For each matched group, the difference of sample means on the dependent (posttreatment) variable (Y) can be discerned from a figure showing regressions of Y on this X, where Y is imperfectly correlated with the pretreatment variable. If the match variable (treatment) has no effect on Y, the regression lines of each matched (or unmatched) group will coincide, as will the Y means. If there is an effect, the result will be non-coinciding, parallel lines with different Y-intercepts; in addition, the samples' Y means will differ, consistent with this effect. In short, it is incorrect to argue that an artifactual regression effect, caused by imperfect correlations (excluding that due to measurement error), biases mean differences between two matched groups.

Appendix B

OUR USE OF DUNCAN'S SOCIOECONOMIC INDEX

As measured using Duncan's socioeconomic index, and as analyzed here along with graduate education and personal income, job status is based on the proportion of the adult white male population in various occupations who have completed a high-school education and who have incomes in excess of $3500 in 1949. Job status may therefore seem little more than a sum of income and education data, and, consequently, may seem to be an inappropriate measure for analyzing the relationships between graduates' current-job status and their income and education. However, there is an important difference between the score assigned to a jobholder on the basis of the educational and income characteristics of the *aggregate* of white males holding that job, and the education or income of *individuals* in that position. Although it is an inaccurate approximation, it may be useful to understand the score as indicating the average educational qualification and financial reward of a position; in contrast, an individual may have more or less education than is normally required for his job, and may earn a great deal more or less than the average income associated with it. Thus, the aggregate basis of Duncan's job-status score contrasts sharply with individual levels of education or income, as those familiar with the ecological fallacy and aggregation problems may appreciate (Robinson, 1950; Hannen, 1972).

Another apparent difficulty is that Duncan's scores are based on data from *white males*; some may thus question their appropriateness for use with data from blacks and/or women. One relevant study (Brown, 1955) found that black job-status ratings were fairly similar to those in NORC studies. Where rankings were dissimilar, the blacks ranked more jobs far below than were above the average NORC ratings for those jobs; however, the jobs rated higher were those in which blacks were overrepresented and into which upwardly mobile blacks tended to move. Similarly, the allocation of job status by both whites and blacks probably varies by age, geographic region, and other characteristics. We can infer from this similarity that if we assigned status scores based on black aggregate data to black individuals, the slight differences in absolute or relative rank of specific jobs would probably not alter significantly the analysis of relationships between these and other variables.

We might also note that an analysis of individual blacks' education, income, and job status that used a job-status measure derived from black aggregate data would be potentially interesting but theoretically different from our study. To use the demographer's jargon, we standardized the jobs of unrepresentative groups of men (some white and some black, most of whom lived in the eastern region of the United States), using a job-status scale based on data from white males and validated with responses from national surveys—that is, we assigned a score without regard to race or region. The reason for this choice was our suspicion that in matters of racial discrimination, what matters is not, for example, whether a black male's income is commensurate with his job's status as derived from education and income data on all black males (or all northern black males) holding the same job. Rather, the crucial question is whether his income is commensurate with his job's status as derived from data on adult white males. (The former approach would probably be more theoretically relevant to, say, a study of a predominantly black city's social organization.)

In short, the appropriateness of our use of Duncan's socioeconomic index is a theoretical matter rather a reflection of uncritical assumptions that blacks completely subscribe to white job-status ratings.

Appendix C

SIGNIFICANCE TESTS_____

Because of the differing extents to which the respective populations of graduates were sampled, significance tests as commonly used were not entirely appropriate for our analyses. The samples of black graduates from ASU and MSU represented rather large proportions of all such graduates (our estimate: at least 80 percent). The sample of Frazier graduates is a far more modest proportion of all Frazier graduates, and the sample of white graduates from ASU and MSU is a very small proportion of all such graduates. Seen in this light, the ASU and MSU black graduates are not so much a sample as an imperfect enumeration of the whole population of such graduates. Our other samples might be correctly termed samples, but with sampling fractions (the ratio of the sample to the population size) that are not negligible.

Ordinary tests of significance assume negligible sampling fractions. Tests can be effectively corrected for nonnegligible fractions, but such corrections require precise knowledge of the actual sampling fractions. Unfortunately, such knowledge lay beyond practical reach. Sampling was done within years of graduation, and the fractions would almost assuredly have been different for each graduating class at each school. Moreover, the relevant population size for the whites and for the Frazier blacks could not be determined by counting all graduates of each class; the relevant populations were rather all graduates who could have matched the ASU and MSU black graduates as well, or nearly as well, as those we interviewed. Enumerating all such graduates, especially the whites, was totally impractical.

The manner in which we chose whites and Frazier blacks for inclusion in this study also departed in some respects from the standards of simple random

181

sampling that are presumed by ordinary significance tests (see Appendix A). This departure was mitigated somewhat by the fact that these graduates were randomly selected, as far as possible, from pools of graduates having grade-point averages and fathers' job-status scores similar to those of the ASU and MSU black graduates; furthermore, the constitutents of these pools were randomly selected from lists of men graduating in each class.

As a result, strictly appropriate—(corrected)—significance tests were not available to us, and ordinarily—(uncorrected)—tests were not as useful as they usually would generally be in protecting our analyses from the effects of sampling variability on our estimates of regression coefficients. However, one can argue that a cautious usage of ordinary tests is still warranted. Campbell (1969), for example, has argued for the utilization of such tests as indicators of the "stability" of estimates, even when they are not strictly appropriate. Moreover, even without knowledge of the actual sampling fractions, we can see that the usual level of significance (.05) is too conservative (even modest sampling fractions—say, .2—can increase the effective significance level of an estimated relationship). Accordingly, for the benefit of readers who would adopt this position, our tables show the coefficients that are significant at both the .10 and .05 levels.

With one exception, we kept our dependence on these tests to a minimum. The exception was that we sometimes applied the criterion of significance to the practical purpose of deciding whether the relationship represented by a regression coefficient was worth specific discussion. Those that survived this first winnowing were then considered in a substantive light, but were still subject to neglect if they ultimately proved very modest and insubstantial. This procedure does not deny the substantive importance of finding that the estimates of some relationships are zero; however, null results are usually noteworthy only when announced expectations to the contrary are disappointed. We were testing too few hypotheses to cover most of our findings, so this situation did not arise frequently.

Appendix D

COMPONENT ANALYSIS_____

In Chapters 4 and 5 we combined the demographic technique of "standardization" (Barclay, 1958) and regression analysis to decompose black-white differences in average personal and family incomes, as well as the difference in the proportion of graduates' wives workiɪ g full time. Using the income decomposition as an example, we begin with two equations (one for white men, one for black), each expressing the mean income ($\overline{\$}$) as a function of several resources (education, years of experience, employment sector, and job status). To simplify this discussion, we confine this illustration to two resources, education (X_1) and years of experience (X_2). The equations for mean black ($\overline{\$}^N$) and mean white ($\overline{\$}^W$) incomes, respectively, are:

$$\overline{\$}^N = a^N + b_1^N \bar{X}_1^N + b_2^N \bar{X}_2^N \tag{D.1}$$

$$\overline{\$}^W = a^W + b_1^W \bar{X}_1^W + b_2^W \bar{X}_2^W \tag{D.2}$$

where a is the income of graduates with zero education and zero experience in each group; b (regression coefficient) denotes the income values of education and experience, respectively; $\bar{X}_1$ and $\bar{X}_2$ are average education and years of experience; and the superscripts N and W denote black and white groups, respectively.

An income gap ($\overline{\$}^W - \overline{\$}^N$) is decomposed by calculating the difference between the appropriate standardized mean incomes and the smaller of the average incomes (usually $\overline{\$}^N$). Standardized income figures are calculated by exchanging either the $\bar{X}$ or the b's between the equations for each group. In our procedure, for example, we first calculate a mean income for blacks by assuming their current income value for education and years of experience, while simultaneously assigning to them the whites' average level of education and experience. The resulting standardized mean income, $\bar{\$}^a$, is equal to:

$$\bar{\$}^a = a^N + b_1^N \bar{X}_1^W + b_2^N \bar{X}_2^W. \tag{D.3}$$

By subtracting this standardized $\bar{\$}^a$ from the average black income, we obtain the *A component*:

$$(\bar{\$}^a - \bar{\$}^N) = b_1^N(\bar{X}_1^W - \bar{X}_1^N) + b_2^N(\bar{X}_2^W - \bar{X}_2^N), \tag{D.4}$$

which indicates that part of the original income gap due to differences in mean black and white educational levels and experience, when the blacks' income value for each resource is held constant.

Second, we hold whites' average education and experience constant and assign the blacks' income values for each resource to whites. If we then calculate a new standardized income $(\bar{\$}^b)$ on this basis and subtract it from the average income for blacks, we obtain the *B component*:

$$(\bar{\$}^b - \bar{\$}^N) = (b_1^W - b_1^N)\bar{X}_1^W + (b_2^W - b_2^N)\bar{X}_2^W. \tag{D.5}$$

The remaining difference $(a^W - a^N$; the *C component*) represents the income difference between whites and blacks with zero education and zero years of experience. Decomposition requires altering the zero point if necessary to obtain meaningful results for particular samples of respondents. Thus in our analysis, the zero point of education for college graduates was set at 16, since by definition, no college graduate has fewer than 16 years of schooling.

In our procedure, the *A component* is the difference in average resources, weighted (multiplied) by blacks' income values (equation D.4); the *B component* is the difference in income values weighted by whites' average resources (equation D.5). Clearly, other procedures, using different weights for components analogous to *A* and *B*, are possible.[1] Consider, for example, a procedure adopted by Duncan (1969) in an earlier example of component analysis. Assuming that blacks' current average resources would remain unchanged, he assigned whites' income values to blacks. He thus derived a different standardized mean income from which to subtract blacks' mean income, and consequently arrived at a different *B* (call it *B′*) *component* than resulted from our procedure. Blacks' average resources could also be assigned to whites, assuming that blacks' resources had income values equal to those of whites. Still another standardized income figure could then be calculated, and so on, yielding a new *A* (call it *A′*) *component*. (The *C component* remains the same for either method.)

We now consider the numerical values resulting from these various components. Let us assume that whites' average resources exceed those of blacks. The differences between A and A', B and B' then depend on which group has resources of greater income value. (We shall assume for the remainder of this discussion that whites have the greater income values, though in some cases, as we saw, whites have the lesser values.) Given this assumption, then A' will exceed A, and B' will be less than B.[2]

The question then arises: How do we choose between these two decomposition methods? Different assumptions underlie each method. There are two possible sources of different, hence distinguishing, assumptions: theoretical explanations of how the income gap arose and how it is presently maintained, and practical policy considerations, that is, steps by which a policy-implementing body could hope to reduce the gap. In reviewing these two sources of assumptions below, we find that alternative theoretical accounts of the income gap do not strictly arbitrate between decomposition methods. Either method could be reasonably adopted by competitive theories. Different policies do correspond, however, to the different methods, though more than one scenario is consistent with any one method.

Theoretical assumptions suggest two possible, and potentially competing, accounts of the income gap. One is racial discrimination. The typically lower income values of blacks' resources (and, hence, the relative size of the B or B' *component*) can be taken as evidence of a structural, competitive advantage for whites. Their education and/or experience are more highly rewarded than are blacks', even when both groups possess the same levels of these resources. This interpretation of the B *component* has been offered in effect by many researchers (Duncan, Featherman, and Duncan, 1968; Michelson, 1968; Duncan, 1969; Coleman, Blum, and Sørenson, 1970). But do unequal income values actually reflect the operation of discrimination? It could also be argued that the uses of education (or the value of experience) differ for, say, "cultural" reasons. The question then becomes: Why this difference? In our study, for example, why should black and white college classmates differ in the income value of their experience since college? Why should the income value of their job statuses differ? In short, why should any two groups of people similarly educated and experienced, and with jobs of comparable status in the same employment sectors, find their prime economic resources dissimilarly valued and rewarded, unless they are being treated unequally in the marketplace? For the present, we see no answer to this basic question that does not lead back to current discrimination, although further research into the uses of education in general, and by blacks and whites in particular, may persuade us otherwise.

The other possible answer lies in the disadvantaged backgrounds or unequal starting points of blacks, which may indicate a residue of discrimination

against blacks' parents, but is not necessarily evidence of current discrimination. This "culture of poverty" perspective was interpreted in this fashion
by Duncan (1969), who therefore proceeded first to calculate that part of the
income gap which reflected differences in average background factors, such as
father's education and job status, number of respondent's siblings, and
respondent's education and job status. We could call such inequalities differences in the social-class level of whites and blacks, and label this interpretation a "class interpretation of racial prejudice" (after Degler, 1969).

According to the criticisms of Duncan (1969) and Michelson (1968), among
others, many researchers and policy makers believe that the entire income gap
is due to unequal backgrounds. Some researchers, including us, believe that
discrimination has combined with disadvantaged backgrounds to produce the
gap, with the latter factor somewhat less important than the former. Either
way, the implied first step in decomposition is to calculate the component due
to average resource differences. Then the *size* of the subsequently calculated B
(or B') *component* speaks to the relative merits of the alternative explanations.
Yet either decomposition method could be reasonably adopted if one wanted
first to calculate the A (or A') *component*. The key question between decomposition methods—which group's weights to use in calculating the
components—is not resolved by researchers' views on the relative impact of
disadvantaged backgrounds versus discrimination.[3]

Turning now to policies for closing the gap, we will continue to presume
that whites' resources have the greater income values. Given this presumption,
there are four possible, workable steps that could be taken, in various combinations: increase the level of blacks' average resources to the average for
whites; increase blacks' income values to those of whites; decrease whites'
average resources to the blacks' average levels; and decrease the income value
of whites' resources to that of blacks. Each decomposition method yields
component values consistent with two different courses of action (by combining
different pairs of steps in different orders). These four policy scenarios are: for
the first method, (1) increase blacks' average resource levels to that of whites',
then increase blacks' income values to equal whites'; (2) decrease whites' income values to the level of blacks', and subsequently decrease whites' average
resource levels to those of blacks. For the second method, (3) increase the
blacks' income values to equal whites', then increase blacks' average resource
levels to equal whites';(4) decrease whites' average resource levels to equal
blacks', and, finally, decrease the income values of whites' resources to equal
those of blacks.

Judging from the apparent tendency of most policy designs to focus on increasing resources of men rather than to tamper directly with the income-value structure, increasing blacks' individual resources, and, hence, their average resource level, is substantially less sociologically and economically intricate, and politically more attractive, than is changing blacks' income values. Decomposition procedures that first calculate the contribution of differences in average incomes, using the blacks' income values as weights (scenario 1 above) need not imply a researcher's agreement with this policy. We assumed this scenario in our analyses simply to give proponents of the disadvantaged-backgrounds theory an opportunity to see clearly the untenability of their assumptions.

We would cite the political impracticality of decreasing average resource levels/income values of either blacks or whites as our justification for dismissing scenarios 2 and 4. This leaves us with scenario 3. Given the results of three of our four decompositions (Chapter 4), our reanalyses of Coleman et al.'s and Duncan's data, and the general finding that whites' resources have greater income value than blacks', decompositions that initially presume the first scenario eventually lead us to the third as the best policy. Of course, if the decomposition of this same gap presumed the third scenario, the components' values would be different. However, for a given difference of income values for a particular set of data, the greater income value of most or all of whites' resources would still indicate that scenario 3 is the most efficient. Assuming that the income values of blacks' resources are less than those of whites at the outset, it simply makes more sense to increase the blacks' resource levels *after*, rather than before, their income value has been increased.

NOTES

1. Another alternative method uses weights consisting of the average value of the two groups' resources for the analogous B *component*, and the average value of the two groups' income values for the analogous A *component*. For a discussion of this approach, as well as the simple derivation of our equations, see Althauser and Wigler (1972).

2. When whites' values are lower, A' will be less than A, and a negative B' will be closer to zero than a negative B.

3. Some might argue that discrimination produces the entire gap. In such a case, there is no reason to begin by calculating that part of the gap due to disadvantaged backgrounds. But even this argument does not imply which set of weights would be consistent with a policy assumed to reduce the income gap.

REFERENCES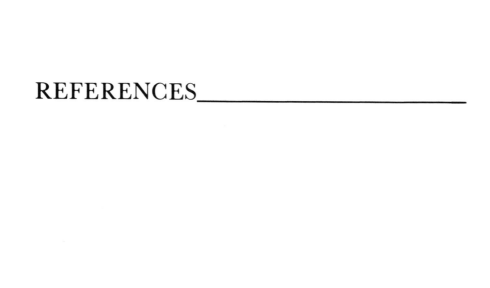

AIGNER, DENIS J.

1970 A comment on problems in making inferences from the Coleman report. *American Sociological Review*, **35**(April):249–252.

ALSOP, JOSEPH

1967 No more nonsense about ghetto education. *New Republic* July:18–23.

ALTHAUSER, ROBERT P., and DONALD RUBIN

1970 Computerized construction of a matched sample. *American Journal of Sociology*, **76**(September):325–346.

1971 Measurement error and regression to the mean in matched samples. *Social Forces*, **50**(December):206–214.

ALTHAUSER, ROBERT P., and MICHAEL WIGLER

1972 Standardization and component analysis. *Sociological Methods and Research*, **1**(August):97–135.

ASHENFELTER, ORLEY

1969 Appendix A. In William G. Bowen and T. Aldrich Finegan, *The Economics of Labor Force Participation*. Princeton, N.J.: Princeton University Press.

ASTIN, ALEXANDER W.

1965 *Who Goes Where to College?* Chicago, Ill.: Science Research Associates Inc.

AXELROD, MORRIS

1956 Urban structure and social participation. *American Sociological Review*, **21**(February):13–18.

BABCHUK, NICHOLAS, and RALPH V. THOMPSON

1962 The voluntary associations of Negroes. *American Sociological Review*, **27**(October):647–655.

BARCLAY, G. W.

1958 *Techniques of Population Analysis*, New York: John Wiley & Sons.

191

BARNOW, B. S.

1972   Conditions for the presence or absence of a bias in treatment effect: Some statistical
       models for Head Start evaluation. *Discussion Paper 122-72.* Institute for Research on
       Poverty.

BECKER, GARY S.

1964   *Human Capital.* New York: National Bureau of Economic Research, Columbia
       Press.

BENHAM, LEE

1971   The labor market for registered nurses: A three-equation model. *The Review of Eco-
       nomics and Statistics,* **53:**246-252.

BEREITER, CARL

1970   Genetics and educability: Educational implications of the Jensen debate. In Jerome
       Hellmuth (ed.), *Disadvantaged Child.* Vol. 3. New York: Brunner/Mazel, Inc. Pp.
       279-299.

BERG, IVAR E.

1970   *Education and Jobs: The Great Training Robbery.* New York: Praeger.

BLALOCK, H. M., JR.

1968   Theory building and causal inferences. In H. M. Blalock, Jr. and Ann B. Blalock
       (eds.), *Methodology in Social Research.* New York: McGraw-Hill. Pp. 115-198.

BLAU, PETER M., and OTIS DUDLEY DUNCAN.

1967   *The American Occupational Structure.* New York: John Wiley & Sons.

BLUM, ZAHAVA D.

1971   Income changes during the first ten years of occupational experience: A comparison of
       blacks and whites. *Report 122.* Baltimore: Center for the Study of Social Organiza-
       tion of Schools, The Johns Hopkins University Press.

1972   White and black careers during the first decade of labor force experience. Part II: In-
       come differences. *Social Science Research,* **1**(September):271-292.

BLUM, ZAHAVA D., and JAMES S. COLEMAN

1970   Longitudional effects of education on the means and occupational prestige of blacks
       and whites. *Report No. 70* (June). Baltimore: Center for the Study of Social Organi-
       zation of Schools, The Johns Hopkins University Press.

BOWMAN, MARY JEAN

1972   Comment. *Journal of Political Economy,* **80**(May-December):S67-S71.

BROOM, LEONARD, and NORVAL GLENN

1965   *Transformation of the American Negro.* New York: Harper & Row.

BROWN, MORGAN C.

1955   The status of jobs and occupations as evaluated by an urban Negro sample. *American
       Sociological Review,* **20**(October):561-566.

CAIN, GLEN G., and HAROLD W. WATTS

1970   Problems in making policy inferences from the Coleman report. *American Socio-
       logical Review,* **35**(April):228-242.

CAMPBELL, ANGUS, GERALD GURIN, and WARREN E. MILLER

1954 *The Voter Decides.* Evanston, Ill.; Row, Peterson and Co.

CAMPBELL, DONALD T.

1969 Reforms as experiments. *American Psychologist,* **24**(April):409–429.

CAMPBELL, DONALD T., and K. N. CLAYTON

1961 Avoiding regression effects in panel studies of communication impact. *Studies in Public Communication,* **3**:99–108.

CAMPBELL, DONALD T., and A. ERLEBACHER.

1970 How regression artifacts in quasi-experimental evaluations can mistakenly make compensatory education look harmful. In Jerome Hellmuth (ed.), *Compensatory Education—A National Debate: Disadvantaged Child.* Vol. 3. New York: Brunner/Mazel, Inc.

CAMPBELL, DONALD T., and JULIAN C. STANLEY

1966 *Experimental and Quasi-experimental Designs for Research.* Chicago: Rand McNally.

CARTER, HUGH, and PAUL C. GLICK

1970 *Marriage and Divorce: A Social and Economic Study.* Cambridge: Harvard University Press. Pp. 169–221.

CHAPMAN, CONSTANCE

1970 The effects of birth order on the success of black and white college graduates. M.A. thesis, Iowa State University.

CHISWICK, BARRY R.

1973 *Income Inequality.* New York: NBER.

CHISWICK, BARRY R., and JACOB MINCER

1972 Time series changes in personal income inequality in the U.S. from 1939, with projection to 1985. *Journal of Political Economy,* **80**(May–June):534–566.

CLARK, KENNETH

1973 Social policy, power and social science research. *Harvard Educational Review,* **43**(February):113–121.

COHEN, BERNARD, and JAN CHAIKEN

1972 Police background characteristics and performance. *Report R-999D01* (August). Rand Corporation.

COLEMAN, JAMES S.

1970 Reply to Cain and Watts. *American Sociological Review,* **35**(April):242–249.

1973 The quality of opportunity and equality of results. *Harvard Educational Review,* **43**(February):120–137.

COLEMAN, JAMES S., CHARLES C. BERRY, and ZAHAVA D. BLUM

1972 White and black careers during the first decade of labor force experience. Part III: Occupational status and income together. *Social Science Research,* **1**(September):293–304.

COLEMAN, JAMES S., ZAHAVA D. BLUM, and AAGE B. SØRENSON

 1970   Occupational status changes for blacks and non-blacks during the first ten years of oc-
        cupational experience. *Report 76.* Baltimore: Center for the Study of Social Organi-
        zation of Schools, The Johns Hopkins University Press.

COLEMAN, JAMES S., et al.

 1966   *Equality of Educational Opportunity.* Washington, D.C.: U.S. Government Printing
        Office.

 1971   White and black careers during the first ten years of work experience: A simultaneous
        consideration of occupational status and income changes. *Report 123.* Baltimore:
        Center for the Study of Social Organization of Schools, The Johns Hopkins
        University Press.

DAVIS, KINGSLEY, and WILBERT E. MOORE

 1945   Some principles of stratification. *American Sociological Review,* **10**(April):242–249.

DEGLER, CARL N.

 1969   The Negro in America—Where Myrdal went wrong. *New York Times Magazine,*
        December:64ff.

DEMERATH, NICHOLAS J.

 1965   *Social Class in American Protestantism.* Chicago: Rand McNally.

DRAKE, ST. CLAIR, and HORACE R. CAYTON

 1962   *Black Metropolis.* Vol. 2. New York: Harper Torchbooks.

DUNCAN, OTIS DUDLEY

 1969   Inheritance of poverty or inheritance of race? In Daniel P. Moynihan (ed.), *On
        Understanding Poverty.* New York: Basic Books. Pp. 85–110.

DUNCAN, OTIS DUDLEY, DAVID LEE FEATHERMAN, and BEVERLY DUNCAN

 1968   *Socioeconomic Background and Occupational Achievement: Extensions of a Basic
        Model.* Washington, D.C.: U.S. Department of Health, Education, and Welfare.

ECKAUS, RICHARD S.

 1973   *Estimating the Returns to Education: A Disaggregated Approach.* Berkeley: The
        Carnegie Foundation.

EDMONDS, RONALD, et al.

 1973   Perspectives on inequality: A black response to Christopher Jencks's *Inequality* and
        certain other issues. *Harvard Educational Review,* **43**(February):76–91.

FARLEY, REYNOLDS, and ALBERT I. HERMALIN

 1971   Family stability: A comparison of trends between blacks and whites. *American Socio-
        logical Review,* **36**(February):1–17.

 1972   The 1960's: A decade of progress for blacks? *Demography,* **9**(August):353–370.

FISHEL, LESLIE H., and BENJAMIN QUARLES, eds.

 1967   *The American Negro: A Documentary History.* Glenview Ill.: Scott, Foresman and
        Company.

FORM, WILLIAM H., and JAMES A. GESCHWENDER

 1962   Social reference basis of job satisfaction: The case of manual workers. *American So-
        ciological Review,* **27**(April):228–237.

FRAZIER, E. FRANKLIN

    1964   *The Negro Church in America.* New York: Schocken Books.

FRIEDMAN, MILTON

    1962   Capitalism and Freedom. Chicago: University of Chicago Press.

GINSBERG, ELI

    1956   *The Negro Potential.* New York: Columbia University Press.

GREELEY, ANDREW, and PETER ROSSI

    1966   *The Education of Catholic Americans.* Chicago: Aldine. Griggs v. Duke Power Co., 915 U.S. 849 (1971).

HAMBLIN, ROBERT L.

    1971   Mathematical experimentation and sociological theory: A critical analysis. *Sociometry,* **34**(December):423–452.

HANNAN, MICHAEL T.

    1972   Problems of aggregation. In H. M. Blalock, Jr. (ed.)., *Causal Models in the Social Sciences.* Chicago: Aldine. Pp. 473–508.

HANOCH, GIORA

    1967   An economic analysis of earnings and schooling. *Journal of Human Resources,* **2**(Summer):310–329.

HANSEN, W. LEE

    1963   Total and private rates of return to investment in schooling. *Journal of Political Economy,* **71**(April):128–140.

HARE, NATHAN

    1965   Recent trends in the occupational mobility of Negroes 1930–1960: An intracohort analysis. *Social Forces,* December:166–173.

HAUSER, ROBERT M., WILLIAM H. SEWELL, and KENNETH G. LUTTERMAN

    1973   Socio-economic background and the earnings of high school graduates. Madison, Wis.: Center for Demography and Ecology, University of Wisconsin.

HINES, FRED, LUTHER TWEETEN, and MARTIN REDFERN

    1970   Social and private rates of return to investment in schooling, by race-sex groups and regions. *Journal of Human Resources,* **5**(Summer):318–340.

HODGE, ROBERT, and DONALD TREIMAN

    1968   Social participation and social status. *American Sociological Review,* **33**(October):722–740.

HOFSTADER, RICHARD, and WILSON SMITH, eds.

    1961   *American Higher Education, A Documentary History.* Chicago: University of Chicago Press.

HYMAN, HERBERT, and CHARLES R. WRIGHT

    1971   Trends in voluntary association memberships of American adults: Replication based on secondary analysis of national sample surveys. *American Sociological Review,* **36**(April):191–206.

JENCKS, CHRISTOPHER

    1973   Inequality in retrospect. *Harvard Educational Review,* **43**(February):138–164.

JENCKS, CHRISTOPHER, and DAVID RIESMAN

1968   *The Academic Revolution.* New York: Doubleday.

JENCKS, CHRISTOPHER, et al.

1972   *Inequality: A Reassessment of the Effect of Family and Schooling in America.* New York: Basic Books.

JENSEN, ARTHUR R.

1969   How much can we boost IQ and scholastic achievement? *Harvard Educational Review,* **39**:1–23.

JOHNSON, CHARLES S.

1938   *The Negro College Graduate.* College Park, Md.: McGrath Publishing Co.

KAYSEN, CARL.

1973   New directions for research. In Lewis C. Salmon and Paul J. Taubman (eds.), *Does College Matter?* New York: Academic Press. Pp. 147–150.

LENSKI, GERHARD E.

1956   Social participation and status crystallization. *American Sociological Review,* **21**(August):458–464.

1961   *The Religious Factor.* Garden City, N.Y.: Doubleday.

LEWIS, SIR ARTHUR

1969   Black power and the American university. *A Princeton Quarterly,* Spring:8–12.

LOGAN, RAYFORD W., ed.

1944   *What the Negro Wants.* Chapel Hill: University of North Carolina Press.

MICHAEL, ROBERT T.

1973   Education in non-market production. *Journal of Political Economy,* **81**(March–April):306–327.

MICHELSON, STEPHAN

1968   *Incomes of Racial Minorities.* Washington, D.C.: Brookings Institution.

1973   The further responsibility of intellectuals. *Harvard Educational Review,* **43**(February):92–105.

MILLER, S. M., and F. REISSMAN

1969   The credential trap. In S. M. Miller and F. Reissman (eds.), *Social Class and Social Policy.* New York: Basic Books. Pp. 69–77.

MILNER, MURRAY

1972   *The Illusion of Equality.* San Francisco: Jossey-Bass.

MINCER, JACOB

1962   On the job training: Costs, returns and some implications. *Journal of Political Economy, Supplement,* October:50–79.

1970   The distribution of labor incomes: A survey with special reference to the human capital approach. *Journal of Economic Literature,* **8**(March):1–26.

OLSEN, MARVIN

1970   Social and political participation of blacks. *American Sociological Review,* **35**(August):682–696.

ORUM, ANTHONY M.

1966   A reappraisal of the social and political participation of Negroes. *American Journal of Sociology*, **72**(July):32–46.

PHILLIPS, DEREK L.

1971   *Knowledge from what? Theories and Methods in Social Research.* Chicago: Rand McNally.

POSNER, JAMES ROBERT

1970   Income and occupation of Negro and white college graduates: 1931–1966. Ph.D. dissertation, Princeton University.

RAINWATER, LEE, and WILLIAM L. YANCEY

1967   *The Moynihan Report and the Politics of Controversy; A Trans-action Social Science and Public Policy Report* [including the full text of *The Negro Family: The Case for National Action*, by Daniel P. Moynihan]. Cambridge, Mass.: MIT Press.

REED, RITCHIE H., and HERMAN P. MILLER

1970   Some determinants of the variation in earnings for college men. *Journal of Human Resources*, **5**(Spring):177–190.

REISS, ALBERT, OTIS DUDLEY DUNCAN, CECIL C. NORTH, and PAUL K. HATT

1961   *Occupations and Social Status.* New York: Free Press.

RIVLIN, ALICE M.

1973   Perspectives on inequality: Forensic social science. *Harvard Educational Review*, **43**(February):61–75.

ROBINSON, WILLIAM S.

1950   Ecological correlations and the behavior of individuals. *American Sociological Review*, **15**(June):351–357.

ROGERS, DANIEL C.

1969   Private rates of return of the United States. *Yale Economic Essays*, **9**(Spring):89–136.

ROSE, ARNOLD

1956   *The Negro in America.* Boston: Beacon Press.

ROTTENBERG, SIMON

1962   The economics of occupational licensing. In *Aspects of Labor Economics.* Princeton: Princeton University Press. Pp. 3–20.

SCHOENBERG, RONALD

1972   Strategies for meaningful comparison. In Herbert L. Costner (ed.), *Sociological Methodology 1972.* San Francisco: Jossey-Bass. Pp. 1–35.

SCHULTZ, THEODORE W.

1960   Capital formation by education. *Journal of Political Economy*, **68**(December):571–583.

SHARP, LAURE M.

1970   *Education and Employment: The Early Careers of College Graduates.* Baltimore: The Johns Hopkins University Press.

SIEGEL, PAUL

1965   On the cost of being a Negro. *Sociological Inquiry*, **35**:41–57.

SIMPSON, RICHARD L.
    1956   A modification of the functional theory of social stratification. *Social Forces,*
           35(December):132–137.

SUTHERLAND, ROBERT L.
    1942   *Color, Class and Personality.* Washington, D.C.: American Council on Education.

TAEUBER, KARL
    1967   White-Negro occupational differentials. *Proceedings of the American Statistical
           Association.* Pp. 254–257.

TAUBMAN, PAUL J., and TERENCE J. WALES
    1973   Higher education, mental ability, and screening. *Journal of Political Economy,*
           81(February):28–55.

THUROW, LESTER
    1967   The occupational distribution of the returns to education and experience for whites
           and Negroes. *American Statistical Association Proceedings.* Pp. 233–243.

    1970   On analyzing the American income distribution. *American Economic Review,*
           60(May):283–285.

    1972   Education and economic equality. *Public Interest,* **28**(Summer): 66–81.

    1973   Proving the absence of positive association. *Harvard Education Review,* **43**(Feb-
           ruary):106–112.

TURNER, RALPH
    1954   Occupational patterns of inequality. *American Journal of Sociology,*
           59(March):437–447.

U.S. BUREAU OF THE CENSUS
    1969   Income in 1967 of persons in the United States. *Current Population Reports, Series
           P-60, No. 60.* Washington, D.C.: U.S. Government Printing Office.

    1971   Differences between incomes of white and Negro families by region, 1969 and 1959.
           Current Population Reports, Series P-23, No. 35. Washington, D.C.: U.S.
           Government Printing Office.

    1971   The social and economic status of Negroes in the United States, 1970. *Current Popu-
           lation Reports, Series P-23, No. 38.* Washington, D.C.: U.S. Government Printing Of-
           fice.

WEISBROD, BURTON, and PETER KARPOFF
    1968   Monetary returns to college education, student ability, and college quality. *Review of
           Economics and Statistics,* **50**(November):491–497.

WELCH, FINIS
    1966   Measurement of the quality of schooling. *American Economic Review,*
           56(May):379–392.

WIGGINS, JAMES A.
    1968   Hypothesis validity and experimental laboratory methods. In H. M. Blalock, Jr. and
           Ann B. Blalock (eds.), *Methodology in Social Research.* New York: McGraw-Hill.
           Pp. 390–427.

WINSBOROUGH, H. M., and PETER DICKINSON

  1971   Components of Negro-white income differences. *Proceedings of the Social Statistics Section of the American Statistical Association.*

WINSBOROUGH, HAL M., E. L. QUARANTELLI, and DANIEL YUTZY.

  1963   The similarity of connected observations. *American Sociological Review,* **28**(December):977–983.

WOHLSTETTER, ALBERT, and SINCLAIR COLEMAN

  1970   Race differences in income. *Report R-578-OEO* (October). Santa Monica: Rand Corporation.

WRIGHT, CHARLES R., and HERBERT H. HYMAN

  1958   Voluntary association memberships of American adults: Evidence from national sample surveys. *American Sociological Review,* **23**(June):284–294.

ZETTERBERG, HANS L.

  1964   *On Theory and Verification in Sociology.* New York: The Bedminster Press.

INDEX

DATE DUE

BRODART, INC.

Cat. No. 23-221